TEMPLES

Circles of Stone

Kaumudi Marathé

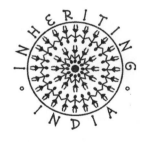

INHERITING INDIA

ESHWAR

About The Author

Kaumudi Marathé is a journalist who writes on architecture, conservation and urban development. She also experiments with fiction. For fun, she writes about risk management and insurance for a business journal.

Marathé lives in Mumbai with her architect husband, Sanjiv Bajaj. When she is not writing, she enjoys Thirkell, the city, long walks, old movies, and cooking for friends.

eESHWAR is an imprint of

BUSINESS PUBLICATIONS INC

A Quartette Group Company

ISBN 81-86982-11-6

Cover design by Sunil Mehta Signatures Mumbai
Illustrations by Srikant Patil
Cover picture reproduced courtesy of Phillips Antiques Mumbai
Processed and printed by Black Dots Mumbai

Published by
ESHWAR
229/A Krantiveer Rajguru Marg
Girgaon, Mumbai — 400 004

CONTENTS

AUTHOR'S NOTE

A great deal of valuable academic material on India's Hindu temples has been collated over the decades by historians, architects and archaeologists. As many shrines have now fallen into disuse or decay, the documentation by people like Percy Brown, James Fergusson, Claude Batley and Stella Kramrisch is crucial to the preservation of India's Hindu architectural heritage.

The sheer number of India's temples, however, means that books on them can rarely be exhaustive. This book does not attempt to be. It is an introduction to readers who are new to the country or the subject. It is a gleaning of information about some of the unusual and representative Hindu shrines across the country.

The history of Hindu temples is inextricably linked to myth and legend. It must be noted that there are innumerable variations of these tales based, among other things, on region, language and cultural background. While every effort has been made to cross-check references for the myths mentioned in the book, some may find that the stories vary from versions they have heard or read previously. This will not be problematic if readers keep in mind that the point is to use these legends to illustrate aspects of Hinduism or narrate anecdotes about specific temples.

A similar note must be made for spellings of both names and other Indian words. It is a subject of great debate which English spelling comes closest to the sound of the original 'Indian' word. I have tried to keep spellings as uniform and phonetically precise as possible — Siva rather than Shiva, Rama rather than Ram - and hope that no sensibilities are offended. The first time an Indian word appears, it is in italics with an English definition in brackets: for example, *mandir* (temple). A complete glossary of the Indian words used in *Temples of India, Circles of Stone,* can be found at the end of the book. If an Indian word is to be pluralized, it appears with the 's' non-italicized: *mandir*-s.

For interested readers, a bibliography has been provided at the back of the book.

A Wayside Shrine

Om, I bow to the holy Vastupurusha of great strength and valour
Whose body rests under all dwellings, Son of Brahma,
Upholder of the entire Universe,
Whose head is placed to carry the burden of the earth,
Who makes all sites [receptacle of] his presence,
The towns and cities, temples [and palaces], houses, tanks and wells,
Who assures all kinds of fulfilment,
Of gracious appearance,
Support of the Cosmos,
Supreme Purusha,
Granter of boons to Indra,
Lord of Dwellings, Obeisance

Pauranikavastusantiprayoga Fol 25

A Wayside Shrine

Om, I bow to the holy Vastupurusha of great strength and valour
Whose body rests under all dwellings, Son of Brahma,
Upholder of the entire Universe,
Whose head is placed to carry the burden of the earth,
Who makes all sites [receptacle of] his presence,
The towns and cities, temples [and palaces], houses, tanks and wells,
Who assures all kinds of fulfilment,
Of gracious appearance,
Support of the Cosmos,
Supreme Purusha,
Granter of boons to Indra,
Lord of Dwellings, Obeisance

Pauranikavastusantiprayoga Fol 25

The Story of a Sacred Land

Once upon a time, legend has it, there lived in the northern kingdom of Kankhol, near the sacred town of Hardwar, a beautiful princess named Sati. Though she had been born as one of the 50 daughters of King Daksha, Sati was really an incarnation of the goddess Parvati. And so when she came of age, she was married to her divine consort, Lord Siva, the Destroyer.

But the curse of a divine garland gifted to King Daksha by the gods, caused him unaccountably to hate his son-in-law. So, one day when he decided to conduct the great Brihaspati *yagna* (sacrifice), he excluded Siva and Sati from the ceremony. His daughter, who loved him dearly, could not stay away and journeyed to Kankhol, thinking, "My father will not be able to turn me away when he sees me." Poor Sati did not comprehend the extent of hardhearted Daksha's anger. When the king saw his child, he spat out a stream of abuses about Siva.

The devoted wife, Sati, was unable to tolerate the insult to her husband. An obedient daughter, she was equally unable to cross her own father. So, consumed by grief, she fell dead before the king. Siva, in his abode on Mount Kailash, heard the sad tidings and flew into a mighty rage, swearing to take revenge on an unrepentant Daksha for his injustice. Coming down to the earth, Siva and his army of spirits marched to the site of the king's *yagna* and decimated Daksha's army. Siva beheaded the monarch and threw his head into the sacrificial fire. Then sorrowfully he picked up Sati's body and wandered with it across the land for many years, aimless and disconsolate.

Lord Vishnu finally took pity on the mighty god and decided to end his mourning. Using his powerful weapon, the *sudarshan chakra* (discus), he cut the corpse into many pieces. As the 51 parts of Sati's body fell to the ground they turned into stone and sanctified the soil upon which they landed, creating 51 holy and potent *pitha*-s or places across India.

And thus it came to be, the ancient Vedic texts tell us, that *Bharatvarsh* (the Indian sub-continent) became a "sacred land" with the holy mountain Meru in the north and the *nav kanyaka*-s (nine maidens) or holy rivers like the Ganga and Yamuna flowing through it. A land of seven *kshetra*-s or regions of active power, the *saptpuri* or seven ancient cities of Ayodhya (Oudh), Mathura, Maya (Hardwar), Kashi (Benares), Kanchi (Kanjivaram), Avantika, and Dvaravati (Dwaraka), where *moksha* (salvation) can be attained. A country which, according to the ancient epic, the *Mahabharata*[1], has thousands of *tirtha*-s (places of pilgrimage) where devotees can ford the river of life and reach the sublime shore beyond.

From its northernmost regions to the tip of its southern peninsula in the Indian Ocean, India is filled with places of worship. It would be difficult to walk a mile here without coming upon a shrine of some sort or the other, be it a historic monument or simply a piece of stone symbolizing a village deity. Each is significant in its own way, commemorating the occasion of a god's visit or deed of valour in the area or explaining its existence due to divine creation or patronage. Everyone wanted to be near god.

For in ancient days, faith meant more than holy tenets to be adhered to, more than a belief in an almighty and powerful being, more than a method to prevent citizens from straying off the straight and narrow. Rather than being a religion, Brahmanism, later known as Hinduism, was a gradual amalgamation of Aryan and Dravidian customs and traditions. God was everywhere, in every person and every object. An all-pervasive force, he ruled, in both subtle and obvious ways, the thought processes, the actions, the consequences, the beliefs, the sciences and the tempo of people's lives.

That Hinduism's influence was strong and consistent is evident in a society where even today this philosophy plays an all-consuming role. It determines matters as worldly as what food is to be cooked in a certain season and when a particular ceremony or rite should be conducted. It also governs matters as spiritual as the nature and attitudes of the Hindu people. Their belief in *karma* (destiny), for instance, which leads to a rather fatalistic view of life. Hindus may traditionally be resigned to events by the belief that it is fate that ordains them and believe, at least in theory, in ultimately sacrificing the material world in favour of asceticism.

In its essence, Hinduism is a way of worshipping life in its every form, and a path towards co-existence. The Hindu looks upon life not as a single opportunity but as part of a larger cycle of births, deaths and deliverance. It is a journey in which death plays a major role but does not result necessarily in *moksha* (liberation). Salvation must be striven for and obtained by various means — *brahmavidya* (knowledge) and *tirtha* (here, the pilgrimage itself), both of which bring *bhakti* (devotion, thus joy). Some people earn it during their life — *jivan mukti,* others spend lifetimes in quest of a final liberation from all forms of existence.

One theory states that the *mandir* (temple) was simply a concrete location given to god for the benefit of those who could not perceive him without help and who could not undertake the most superior form of pilgrimage, the *manastirtha* (pilgrimage of the mind), whose "deep, clean water is truth (*satya*)."[2] The concept of the temple intended for the uplift of the common man works in abstract. However, as religious architecture evolved, the shrine with all its inherent significance, became a symbol of power and wealth with dynasties vying against each other to create more magnificent, more memorable edifices. While these may have served to immortalize their names, in reality, patrons and administrators often discriminated against the vast majority of the population, serving only a privileged elite.

The skeleton of Hinduism, without the complications of

politics of caste and power however, is pantheistic, for two reasons. The first is the belief that though there is but one Supreme Lord, he takes on many forms for different purposes — to preserve good, destroy evil, restore peace on earth, and vanquish chaos. As these myriad forms benefit humanity in innumerable ways, they must all be worshipped. Secondly, derived as it is from ancient fertility rites and the worship of natural powers such as the sun, moon, stars, tides, water, fire, and air, Hinduism preserves the human personifications of these powers even to this day, in the form of their deities — Surya, Soma, Ganga, Agni, Vayu, Varuna and others. Indeed, as many as 33 Vedic deities have been incorporated into Hinduism, worshipped either in small cults or nationally.

The holy trinity of gods derived from the Vedic period includes Brahma, the Creator; Vishnu, the Preserver; and Mahesh (Siva), the Destroyer; and paradoxically, also the Protector. According to Hindu mythology, Brahma, though the greatest of all gods, was once cursed that he would have no followers and that no memorials would be built to him. This explains why there are very few *mandir*-s devoted to him, though he appears as a subsidiary god in the shrines of others. While not worshipped, Brahma remains highly venerated.

The chief deities of the Hindus are the remaining members of the trinity, Vishnu and Siva. Their followers form the two key sects of Hinduism, the Saivite group of Siva and the Vaishnavite of Vishnu. Although each worships their own god, the link between the two is so convoluted and intertwined that inevitably when one is being worshipped, the other will be too. A shrine of Vishnu, for instance, would contain idols of other gods, including Siva or his wife Parvati. Indeed most temples, regardless of whom they are dedicated to, will possess an image of Siva's son Ganesha, the elephant god, for all good deeds are supposed to begin with an invocation to him.

A whole range of lesser gods and goddesses are also worshipped by Hindus, in individual shrines or in conjunction with the great ones. Some of the 10 *avatar*-s (incarnations) of Vishnu, sent to the earth to vanquish evil, are worshipped in their own right. Others are respected and depicted in many temples.

These *avatar-s* are Matsya (fish), Kurma (tortoise),

A View of Kashi on the Ganga

A View of Kashi on the Ganga

Varaha (boar), Narasimha (man-lion), Vamana (dwarf), Parasurama (Brahmin warrior), Rama (the ideal man), Krishna (the dark-skinned god), Buddha (the Hindu clergy, in an attempt to adapt to changes brought about by the newer religion of Buddhism, converted its chief source into an *avatar*), and Kalkin (an amorphous *avatar* yet to appear). Of these, Krishna and Rama acquired the status of great gods, even eclipsing Vishnu and Siva in popularity, largely because of their tangible human form and qualities, including quirks and failings, and because their stories narrated in the *Mahabharata* and *Ramayana* epics[3] were those that devotees could identify with.

While Siva and Vishnu remained in heaven, only occasionally coming down to the earth, Rama and Krishna were born here, the former brought up to be king, the latter supposedly a cowherd (often depicted with a cow, and playing a flute to entice his herd home), living and dying as mortal beings.

In pre-Aryan and Aryan times, the mother goddess had been a consequential figure symbolizing fertility and birth, aspects of life that were deemed sacrosanct. The fact that the innermost sanctuary of all Hindu temples is called the *garba grha* (place of the womb and, therefore, the sanctum sanctorum), is testimony to this reverence. The mother goddess was worshipped by several indigenous 'primitive' cults, including the Tantric which overlaid this worship with sexual connotations.

However, with the coming of the patriarchal Aryan invaders, the prominence of the mother goddess gradually declined. Various aspects of womanhood — the meek, the brave, the angry — are still respected in Hinduism but the female deity usually holds a subordinate place to the male. Lakshmi, wife of Vishnu, is the goddess of wealth, good fortune and beauty; Saraswati of learning; Parvati is the perfect wife; and Durga epitomizes the female element of life.

In attendance on all the major gods are their servants and vehicles, images of which also appear in shrines, frequently being given separate altars as well. These attendants are often symbolic of the particular characteristics of the deities, their preferences of abode, or the areas of life and earth that they control. So Siva rides a bull, Nandi, virile and strong; Vishnu, a serpent, Naga; and Ganesha, a mouse or bandicoot.

Surya drives a chariot pulled by seven horses, the subject of many carvings in Hindu temples, and Yama, the god of death, is seated upon an awe-inspiring black buffalo. Lakshmi, who was recovered from the ocean by a tortoise, is often depicted standing upon one, as is Ganga, the river goddess. Saraswati glides about on a *saras* (swan) from which she derives her name while the warrior goddess Durga or Kali, rides a ferocious tiger.

As is only natural in a religion which has developed, adapted, and been built upon over millennia, Hinduism is now not only a mélange of anecdotes and moral tales about divine beings and interventions but also a convoluted, often rigid, sometimes incomprehensible collection of traditions, ceremonies, rituals, and forms of worship. Some of these are obsolete or followed unquestioningly or without knowledge. The 'way of life' has in many ways turned into another cliché, 'blind faith'.

Notes

1 It is difficult to date the epic *Mahabharata*, historians say, but it was probably written around the early to middle parts of the last millennium, B.C.

2 *The Hindu Temple*, Stella Kramrisch, University of Calcutta, 1946

3 The *Ramayana* was written around the early to middle parts of the last millennium, B.C., a little later than the *Mahabharata*

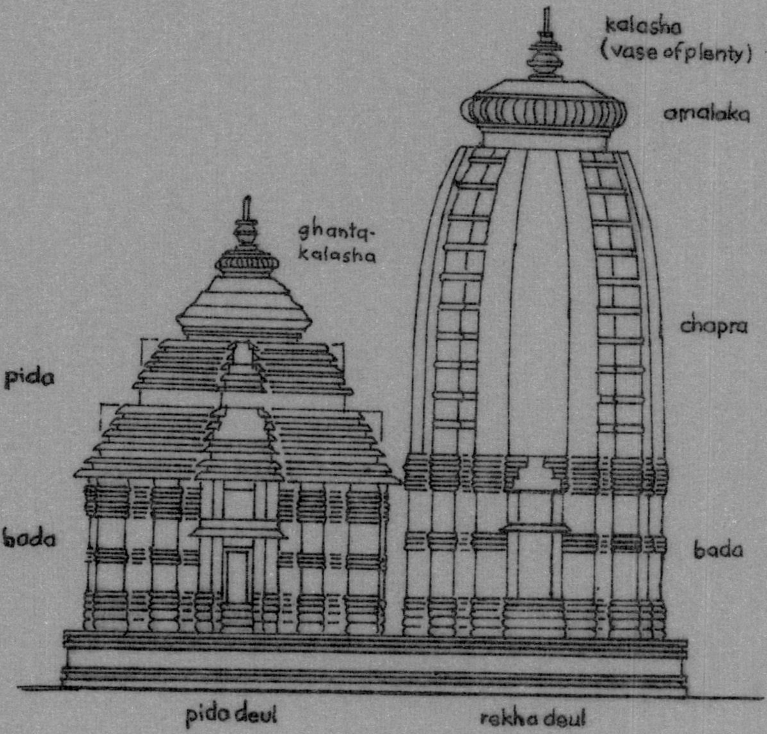

Elevation and Plan of An Orissan Temple

The Temple is made up of the presence of Siva *and* Sakti *and of the Principles and all Forms of manifestation from the elementary substance, Earth, to* Sakti. *The concrete form of* Siva *is called House of God. Hence one should contemplate and worship it.*

Isanasivagarudadevapaddhati
Pt. III
Chapter XII.16

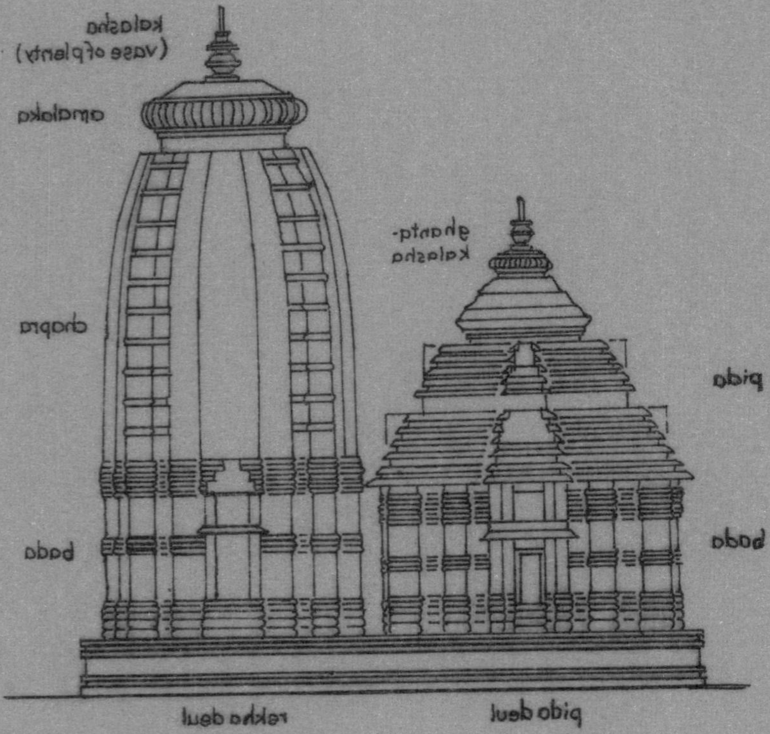

Elevation and Plan of An Orissan Temple

The Temple is made up of the presence of Siva and Sakti and of the Principles and all Forms of manifestation from the elementary substance, Earth, to Sakti. The concrete form of Siva is called House of God. Hence one should contemplate and worship it.

Isanasivagarudadevapaddhati
Pt. III
Chapter XII.16

The Place of the Womb

This land is teeming with temples — both miniature and monumental, stark and ornate, stretching from beyond the borders of what is today known as India, from as far west as Harappa to as far east as Bansberia, from Pandrethan in Kashmir to the temple of Kanyakumari in Tamil Nadu. The house of the Hindu god is the form of Indian architecture most written about but the one that, paradoxically, has defied complete definition.

Variously called *vimana* (well proportioned), *prasada* (seat of the Lord), *devalaya* (house of God), *devagram* (the village of God), and *sthana* or *sthanam* (the holy place), a Hindu temple is usually all of these things. It is a celebration of rites and traditions; a highly evolved art form; a panorama of myths and legends for the entertainment and enlightenment of the devotee; a record of contemporary life and values; a depiction of natural powers (such as the planets and stars, the changing of seasons, and symbolic animal spirits); a tool to uplift the worshipper's soul; a symbolic presentation of the aspects of good and evil, birth and death, worldly and divine, mortal and immortal; a social and cultural centre; and a spectacular display of political and economic power, both in town and country.

The temple was the economic core around which towns evolved. Its construction and maintenance provided people with jobs and allied professions while its gods blessed and guarded them. They, in turn, honoured their images with the appropriate veneration, care, and service. The importance of the sacred role of temples in uniting people with god made these institutions powerful and rich, enabling them to play a large role in the other functions of the village or town, whether judicial, moral or educational.

Temples had a philanthropic role to play as well. People were sometimes fed there free of cost, pilgrims were sheltered in their *dharamshala*-s (accommodations specially built within temple complexes for visiting pilgrims), and they often had schools attached to them. Beggars till today continue to eke out a living from alms in temple yards. Though the tradition of education at a holy shrine hardly exists now, it is prevalent in Indian Islam where the mosque has, attached to it, a *madarsa* (primary school) for young children.

At its most fundamental, a temple was the embodiment of peace and purity, a sanctuary from the world of chaos outside, where god met man and where man could escape from the confusion of his earthly world and return to the safety and sanctity of the womb.

FROM BURIAL MOUNDS TO SACRED SITES
The Origin Of Temple Architecture In India

The ultimate origin of the Hindu temple is said to be the ancient "crude circle of stones within which man enshrined sacred relics, human or divine. To cap them and mark the holy spot he used a cap-stone which has its counterpart in the *shikhara* or spire of the fully developed temple."[1] From Vedic times (1500-700 BC), there had been a tradition of religious architecture. Texts on the subject began to appear around the same time period. However, construction was presumably on a small and localized scale, utilizing easily perishable materials like timber, plaster, brick, mud and clay, which lacked the permanence and grandeur of stone. Indeed, during this stage of Hinduism's evolution, and according to Vedic texts, brick took ritual precedence over stone.

The emperor Asoka who ruled from the magnificent Pataliputra in the Gangetic basin of Central India, is credited with ordering the construction of the first significant stone structures in India in the 3rd century BC. These were *chaitya*-s or large rock-cut temples for the worship of the Buddha; *stupa*-s or commemorative receptacles of his relics; rock-edicts which proclaimed the laws of the land; and superbly formed and polished pillars in stone that were erected across the kingdom.

What his grandfather Chandragupta Maurya, father Bindusara and he himself had done, was to not only conquer a huge region of the Indian subcontinent but to bring together those vanquished territories and meld them for a considerable length of time into one large kingdom. The Mauryan empire was the first of note in the country's history. In the largely agrarian economy of the north, rulers established order, consistency and control by instituting an impressive administration system, dividing territories into manageable districts, and formulating rules for taxation, commerce, the pricing of goods, guilds, and providing such amenities as irrigation canals and dams.

Their far-sighted approach generated a feeling of security among their subjects. In such an atmosphere, the arts were bound to flourish. Even had they not, Asoka, in a single-minded and zealous manner, had indirectly promoted them in his attempts to spread the word of the Gautama Buddha far and wide. Thus, India's imperial art form was also its first religious one. However, after the decline of the Mauryan empire, the various parts of the northern segment of the sub-continent were ruled by lesser dynasties.

The next 'nationally' powerful rulers were the Guptas, who reigned from about the 4th to the 7th centuries AD, and whose power saw the re-emergence of great religious construction paralleled by a similar boom in southern India. This period, often called the Classical or Golden Age (considered by many to be a fallacy), was a time when the arts prospered and architecture especially received strong encouragement. Certainly, the post-Gupta period in India was one where, across the country, acclaimed temple building occurred.

VASTUPURUSHAMANDALA

The Vastupurushamandala, the diagram of a temple is a yantra (spell). *It is an artifice in which the bhumi* (ground) *is converted into the extent of the manifested universe.*[2]

According to tradition, the design of any Hindu temple, or indeed any Hindu structure, anywhere in the country, at any time, is to be based on the fundamental principle of the *Vastupurushamandala*. An amalgamation of the laws of astronomy, astrology and mathematics, it is depicted by a square, the faultless form, representing a sense of order and perfection in direct contradistinction to the turmoil present in human existence. Within the square is inscribed a circle. This is symbolic of the Hindu theory that life is cyclical, consisting of movement from birth to death and back again.

The *Vastupurushamandala* expresses in one small diagram not only the crux of Hindu philosophy but also the distribution of the gods and stars in relation to human beings. Each has its own designated space, beginning with Brahma, the Creator, in the centre, and moving outwards to the lesser gods. Thus, in the symbolic centre or sanctum, both worshipper and God exist side by side.

It must be made clear, however, that the traditional theory of *Vastupurushamandala* is distinctly different from the fad of pseudo-scientific babble about *Vastu* architecture circulating in India today. A lack of cohesive and appropriate architecture in the country and the widespread gossip that a *Vastu* building will bring better luck to its owners or users, has increased the demand for such structures. In this scenario, *Vastu* has not escaped corruption, with '*Vastu* specialists' springing up all over India and many designers seeing the trend as a means to making big money from emotionally needy clients.

The text of the *mandala* states clearly that the temple stands in space, direction-less, and therefore should not possess any one special façade. At the same time it defines the position to be accorded to various structures in the temple complex, where its buttresses were to be built, and where doors, beams, and windows could or could not be placed.

WHERE TO BUILD A TEMPLE

Since the temple was to be the house of god, it had to be erected in a place that was suitable to him and conducive to his contentment. Its inviting nature or the actual function of refuge from hard life outside also suggests that man's contentment formed part of the intention of the design. Temples have been built at diverse locations in India, on craggy mountain tops, in valleys and plains, on islands, by the banks of rivers, in forts, near forests, at the heart of cities, and distant from any civilization. This may seem illogical but as one ancient text explains, "The gods always play where groves are near, rivers, mountains and springs, and in towns with pleasure gardens... it is (in) such places that the gods love and always dwell in."

No matter where it is situated, one essential factor for the existence of the temple is water. For water is a purifying element and even if not available in reality, must be present in symbolic representation. Water is central to the economy and to the perpetuation of any civilization. In Hinduism, therefore, water was highly revered. The stipulation of a water body at a temple site ensured respect for the substance and a location that was favorable for construction and maintenance. Needless to say it attracted and served devotee and passerby equally.

OF THE ORDERING OF CHAOS

Temples are built where tirthas are; their towering shapes to the last point of their height teem with form and have the urge and fullness of Indian nature; step by step, level by level, they lead the eye of the devotee from this world to the worlds above.[3]

In the Hindu religion, worship is not so much about congregations as it is about individual prayer. The way the temple is designed reflects the need of each person to reach god. Based on the *Vastupurushamandala*, the basic temple is square in plan, its most significant component being the *garba grha*, with all the other chambers being purely additive. Yet, this part is the one that is reached last by the devotee for he is led into it by a progression of architectural, sculptural and symbolic devices so that by the time he arrives there he is in a state of mind befitting worship.

The rules for the construction of the temple are laid down in ancient architectural treatises such as the *Vastu Sastra* or the ‘science of architecture’[4]; the *Brhat Samhita*, compiled by Varahamihira in the mid-sixth century AD and based on the works of legendary architects like Manu and Visvakarma; and the *Mayamata*. Much of the rationale for the guidelines laid down by these great craftsmen is culled from the holy texts of Hinduism; the four *Veda*-s — *Rig, Atharva, Yajur* and *Sama*[5]; the numerous *sastra*-s (in this case, treatises; also science) written through the ages on various subjects; the *Purana*-s;[6] and the *Upanishad*-s.[7]

The *garba grha* is usually surrounded by a *pradakshina* path (circumambulatory path) which may be built repetitively many times around the exterior of the temple, the whole complex, and the subsidiary shrines. The devotee, walking around the shrine in a clockwise direction, symbolically encircles the universe. To enter the *garba grha* he makes his way, usually along a single axis, from the entrance staircase to the portico, thence into a hall; closed or simply pillared, a *mandapa* (usually the main hall).

Beyond and directly in front of him, whose line of vision is directed by rows of flanking pillars, is the altar. Before he reaches it, however, he may have to cross more than one *mandapa*, utilized for related congregational activities such as ritual offering, feeding of the poor, dancing and music, and the singing of *bhajan*-s (hymns or religious songs) every day, at stipulated times, or during special festivals or sacred occasions.

Contemporary pastimes like hunting and wrestling, to name a few, were recorded. Of much significance were the tableaux depicting the patron of the temple and recounting his bravery, largesse and devotion to god. There was almost no aspect of life, religious or otherwise, that did not find its way onto the walls, windows, doors, beams, roofs, niches, ceilings, pillars and spires of the temple. While Western architecture sought more and more to expose the structure of a building, the Hindu tradition aimed at masking it beneath a profusion of stone splendour. While the sculpture of the former was largely abstract in design, the Indian sculptor drew upon the world he saw and experienced for use in his art.

The beauty of the stone was far less important than the

creation of the artist. However, this is not to say that the profusion of carvings in Hindu temples was over-enthusiastic, arbitrary or unplanned. Every curve and figure was positioned with care and precision, laden with symbolism and purpose while in the Western world, carving was restricted to only certain elements of religious architecture.

Contrasted sharply with the decorative outer parts of the Hindu temple was the bare, plain, dark sanctum. Framed within the doorway, where any embellishment had ended, the idol stood free of distracting elements, so that all the senses of the pilgrim could be centred upon him. His power was so strong and his beauty so divine that no adornment was necessary. Often, however, the generosity of the patron extended itself to providing expensive jewellery and rich silk apparel for the deity.

The essential water body of the temple is present generally in the form of a well or *kund* (tank) placed to the west of the shrine or in front of it. The temple complex may also contain cells or cloisters for its priests and subsidiary shrines devoted to the supreme deity's consort, attendant, or vehicle. Energy radiates in all directions from the divine image in the *garba grha*, and at those points of power, lesser shrines are situated.

In the *panchayatana* temple (a five shrined complex), for instance, the central structure is surrounded by one at each of its corners, at the cardinal points signifying five holy spots in all. At other sites, where only one altar had been planned, it was not unlikely to have sanctums spring up randomly wherever there was space when wealthy devotees donated money for them. The other vital structures on the temple estates were its kitchens, store rooms, libraries and treasuries, but little information seems to be available on them as they tended to be functional and artistically undistinguished.

The history of India is roughly classified into three rather broad periods by historians. The classical age from 400 BC to the 7th or 8th century AD, the medieval from the 8th to the 12th centuries AD, and the Sultanate period from the 12th century to the period of the British Raj. Over the first three periods, two major styles of temple building had evolved; the *Nagara* or metropolitan (fashionable) style was northern and the *Dravida* belonged to the south.

The basis for both were the same architectural texts. While the Nagara style was highly varied because its wide territory meant regional modifications and repeated invasions meant destruction and rebuilding, the Dravida was more cohesive. The preponderance of shrines in this tradition is spread over a smaller area than in the north and being geographically better sheltered from external factors, appears more uniform and well defined than its Nagara cousin.

The earliest temples of both styles were mere adaptations of the predominantly wooden structures that had preceded them. This is made abundantly clear if one looks at the *chaitya-s* of the Mauryans, hewn from caves but duplicating wooden framework, arches and window details in the rock.

The structure of the spire differentiates one style from another, apart from traditions of embellishment that generally reflect not just these two styles but the vernacular background of the artist as well. The Nagara spire is vertical or curvilinear and continues the lines of the walls below it and meets at a point over the sanctum. The Dravida one is a high, pyramidal superstructure, divided into storeys, and crowned with a polygonal dome. A third variation, the Vesara style, was a sub-category of the Dravida, employing a round dome.

SCULPTURE

Temple sculpture is a highly organized and sophisticated art form created in various ways for the dual purpose of embellishing and narrating. It exists in temples as free-standing figures or in friezes, on brackets, columns, lintels, pediments, borders, cornices, spires, horizontal bands, vertical sections, moldings and *torana*-s (garland, gateway, door ornamentation).

The human figure is often the model for statues of gods but precise rules were laid down in the ancient architectural texts for the dimensions and proportions that sculptors had to follow when creating images of certain types of *deva*-s (gods), *apsaras*, or *asura*-s (demons). Apart from this, they employed local art forms and relied on their collective memory for the figures and faces of divinities. The figure of the Sun in certain

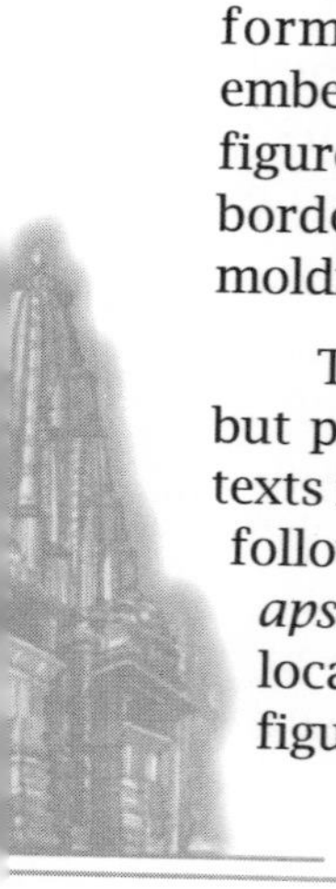

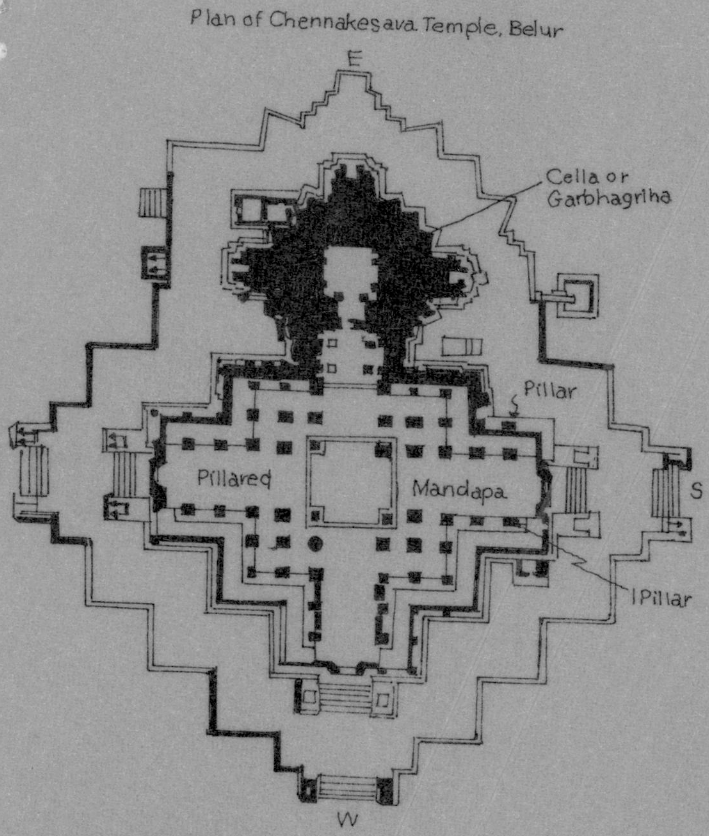

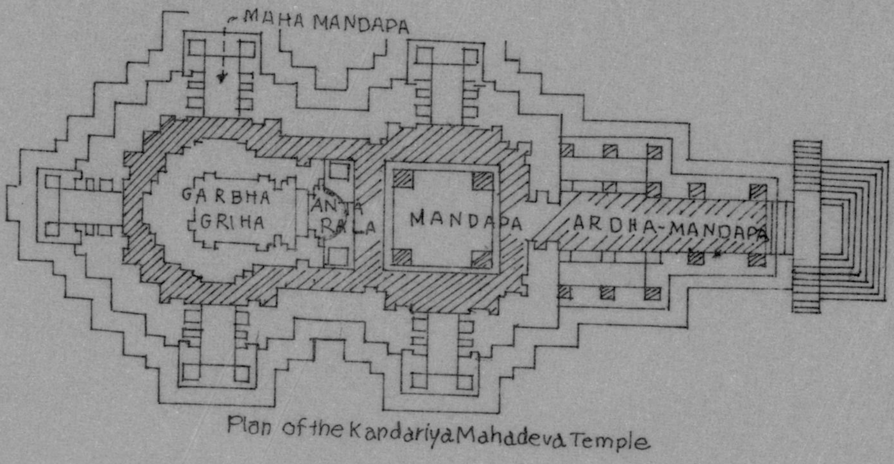

Differing Flatplans of a Northern and a Southern Temple

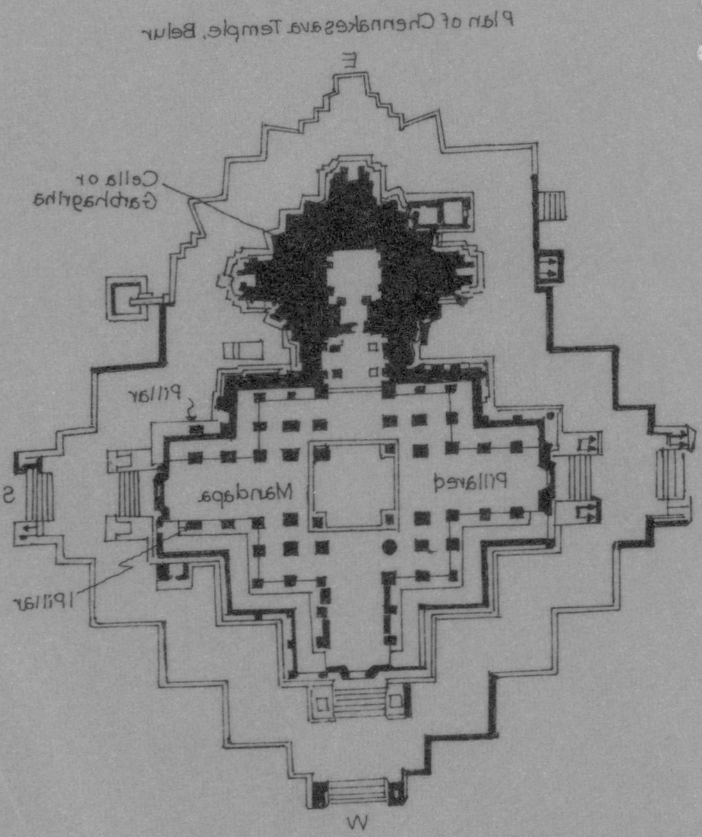

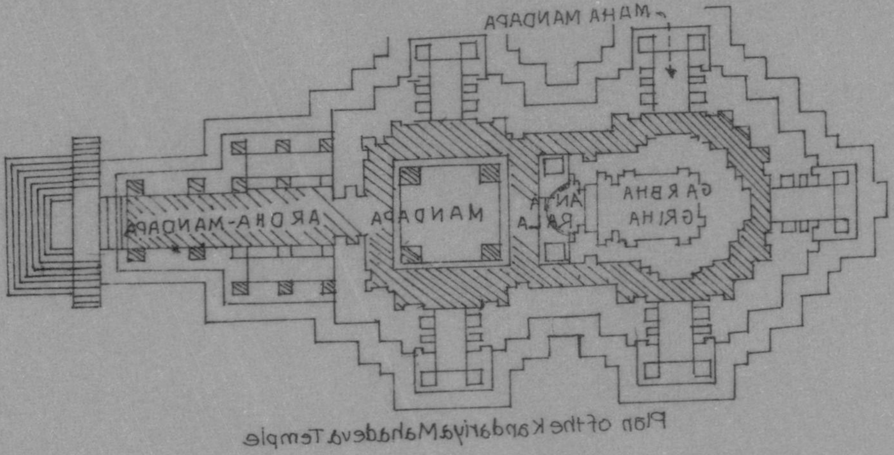

Differing Flatplans of a Northern and a Southern Temple

northern temples therefore, dressed in cloak and boots, is obviously derived from foreign cultural elements in the region while his demeanour and facial features at the Sun Temple of Konark in Orissa are distinctly indigenous.

Gods are represented in the two basic aspects of being - *santa* (the benign or peaceful) and *ugra* (the enraged or terrific) — and display certain states of mind, the range of feelings being classified as the nine emotions (*nav rasa*). These are held to be *srngara* (erotic), *hasya* (laughing), *karuna* (pathetic), *vira* (heroic), *raudra* (furious), *bhayanaka* (fearful), *bibhatsa* (loathsome), *adbhuta* (supernatural), and *santa* (peaceful).

Guidelines indicate the stance of each figure, depending on his role and position in the divine hierarchy. There are four basic stances — the *samabhanga*, where the weight of the body is evenly balanced, *abhanga* (a slight bend), *tribhanga* (triple bend), and *atibhanga* (excessive bend).

Their bodies are youthful, suggesting immortality, their figures, whether shaped floridly or simply, seem suffused with an ethereal quality. Their young faces are ageless, with forehead, eyebrows, eyes, nose, lips being precisely distributed, uniform and often stylized. Nevertheless they are an indication of the region of their creation.

The treatises define certain lengths of face and body — *nava* or *dasa tala*-s (nine or ten lengths) — for the gods and goddesses, but the perfect proportion is described as follows: "The height from the soles of the feet up to the root of the hair on the forehead is equal to the width between the tips of the middle fingers when the arms are stretched horizontally."[8] Thus, while the holy trinity would be carved in *dasa tala*-s, goddesses would be one length less (*nava tala*-s) while the Vamana or dwarf *avatar* of Vishnu would be only seven.

WORSHIP

Pooja (worship) in the Hindu tradition takes the form of a personal prayer and communion with god and the intervention, on the individual's behalf, by the priests versed in the rituals and ceremonies associated with various deities and occasions. The prayer encompasses not just a silent fellowship with the divine being but a ritual of chants and verses used to propitiate or invoke him. The live temple is full of activity, with the deity needing regular care. The idol is ritually bathed, clothed, bejewelled, showered with flowers, fed, entertained, and even married.

Various mortal ceremonies also take place on the temple estate. Wedding vows taken in front of god, for instance, are considered sacred even if there has been no elaborate ceremony and traditional purifying fire. Symbolic sacrifices are made here by those seeking a boon or divine intervention. At the Tirupathi temple in Andhra Pradesh, dedicated to Vishnu (or Sri Balaji, as he is known in the south), hordes of pilgrims flock every day for it is said that the deity grants anything asked of him. In return they sacrifice their hair to him.

While the emphasis may be on individual fellowship, community worship does take place in the form of gatherings to sing hymns or observe priests conducting the daily rituals. People also gather at the temple or local meeting halls to celebrate special occasions.

Festivals

The Hindus follow a lunar calendar and their festivals or holy days therefore shift, from year to year, in relation to the Gregorian calendar. Hindu festivals had their beginnings in both Vedic and Dravida (or later) traditions and were based on seasonal changes, the honouring of professional occupations, occasions of thanksgiving, religious observances, the movements of the planets and stars, the commemoration of important events in Hindu lore or a combination of these.

In the olden days, festivals provided an interlude from the humdrum of life or entertainment in the form of song and dance, ritual, good food, and gatherings of loved ones. Weddings too were anticipated just as keenly. Lasting a month or more, from preparation to celebration, they were a welcome change from the monotony of daily life.

Hindu observances would be too many to count or list. Nonetheless, some of the chief festivals or holy days that Hindus all over India celebrate or observe, include (from

January to December), Makar Sankranti, Sivaratri, Holi, Rama Navami, Rakhi, Janmashtami, Ganesha Chaturthi, Dusserah, and Diwali.

Notes

1 *The Temples of North India*, Publications Division, Ministry of Information and Broadcasting, India, 1959

2 Early Buddhist stone construction probably carried over some of the characteristics of previous, less permanent Hindu architecture, then itself came to be imitated in later Hindu temples across India.

3 *The Hindu Temple*, Stella Kramrisch, University of Calcutta, 1946

4 The *Vastu Sastra* also lays down rules for the construction of other buildings, and town planning

5 There are four *Veda*-s or Vedic texts; the *Rig*, *Atharva*, *Yajur*, and *Sama*. "Our earliest literary source is the *Rig Veda*, parts of which were originally composed prior to 1,000 B.C. The remaining Vedic literature (the other 3 *Veda*-s) is of later date." *The History of India*, Romila Thapar, Volume I, Penguin India, Calcutta, 1990. The word Veda derives from the Sanskrit *vid* – to know. The *Rig Veda* consists of 1028 hymns to various deities and is the oldest religious text in the world.

6 As opposed to the Vedic literature, the *Purana-s* contains traditional history and lore, collected in the millennium from 500 B.C. to 500 A.D.

7 The *Upanishad-s* are mystic Vedic verses composed from c. 700 B.C. onwards

8 *The Hindu Temple*, Stella Kramrisch, University of Calcutta, 1946

The Sun Temple ~ Martanda

Ranaditya built at the village of Simharotsika a [temple of] Martanda which became famous everywhere under the name of Ranapurasvamin.

That liberal [king, Lalitaditya-Muktapida] built the wonderful [shrine] of Martanda with its massive walls of stone within a lofty enclosure and its town swelling with grapes.

Rajtarangini
~ Kalhana

The Sun Temple - Martanda

Ranaditya built at the village of Simharotsika a
[temple of] Martanda
which became famous everywhere under the
name of Ranapurasvamin.

That liberal [king, Lalitaditya-Muktapida] built
the wonderful [shrine] of Martanda with its
massive walls of stone within a lofty enclosure
and its town swelling with grapes.

Rajtarangini
- Kalhana

The Abode of Gods

The Temples of the North

Martanda — Surya; **Pandrethan**, **Avantipur** — Avantiswamin, Avantiswara, **Badrinath**, **Amarnath**, **Kedarnath**

The snow-bound, mountainous regions of Kashmir, the northern-most, and now politically turbulent, state of India, have always held a mystical appeal for Indians. The Himalayas were the abode of innumerable Hindu gods but most specially of the stern Siva, who resided on Mount Kailash with his wife. She too belonged to the Himalayas, as her name Parvati (woman of the mountains) implies.

These steep peaks have been shrouded in sacred aura for eons. Partly because of their inaccessibility, they have always been a source of mystery and legend. Pilgrims, sages and saints have gone there in search of divine deliverance. The heroes of the *Mahabharata* are said to have done penance in the region, ultimately rising up to heaven from these mountains. The 7th century philosopher Swami Shankaracharya, travelled here all the way from Kerala, over 3,000 miles, on a pilgrimage.

The culture of Kashmir has always been self-sustaining. It has a different climate, topography, and way of life from the rest of the country. Due to the difficulties inherent in reaching the state, there was less commerce and interaction between Kashmir and the civilization farther south in the Gangetic plains. Therefore less influence, whether in the fields of art, literature or architecture, filtered there from the cradle of Indian civilization.

It is thought that Kashmir belonged to the vast kingdom of King Asoka and that it was he who built the city of Srinagar. Be that as it may, the Mauryan civilization made no lasting effects upon it. Kashmir came into its own, probably around the 7th century AD under King Lalitaditya's reign, with the conquest of northern Punjab. At this time, the political situation also in the hilly territory had stabilized due to the availability of cultivable land, created by the construction of many dams and embankments, preventing migration into the southern valleys.

The civilization was at its peak from then on, for about three centuries more. It was around this time that its most well known temples, the Surya temple at Martanda, the Siva and Vishnu shrines at Avantipur and the better preserved but smaller Siva temple at Pandrethan were built. Kashmir's temple architecture followed its own vernacular pattern, with quasi-classical elements, but greatly determined by its climatic conditions and style of secular construction.

Today, unfortunately, very few ancient temples are intact in the area. Many were destroyed after the 10th century by Muslim invaders. Sites were then denuded and the materials reused for new construction. Any remains have suffered centuries of weathering. The few structures that exist, in varying stages of ruin, are homogeneous in a style that saw little innovation after its origin around the 6th or 7th century.

The Hindu religious architecture of Kashmir was mostly Saivite. However Vaishnava temples and Buddhist shrines were also constructed. A telling story about King Avantivarman, who built the temples at Avantipur, is recalled by the historian Kalhana in his renowned 12th century text, the *Rajtarangini.* It indicates the religious tolerance of the local people. Apparently, the sovereign was a devout Vaishnava. But his trusted general Sura, prayed to Siva. So, in deference to

Sura's choice, all his life Avantivarman also worshipped Sura's god, only admitting on his deathbed "the attachment to the worship of Vishnu, which he had long hidden."

The temples of Kashmir, reflect the climate of the region with their pitched (sloping) roofs designed to drain off rain or snow easily, and their wooden-style detail echoed in stone. They also stand testimony, through their temple sculpture, to the influence of the neighbouring province, Gandhara, where Byzantine and Greek artisans had employed a Mediterranean form. Visible too, in the horseshoe style windows, reminiscent of *chaitya-s*, and the cells to accommodate priests, are elements of Buddhist architecture, brought to the region by earnest proselytizers. They, because of King Asoka's missionary zeal, had travelled all over the continent spreading the word of the Buddha.

Generally constructed within city limits, temples were laid out in the middle of oblong courtyards that were enclosed by 'running cells' or chapels with long, narrow, pillared verandahs in front of them. The temples were once topped by gabled roofs rather like those seen atop modern houses in the area. The sculptures at Martanda, Pandrethan and Avantipur, the delicacy of intricate embellishment details, and the features of the carved figures, bespeak the effect that early Greek invaders had on the art and architecture in Kashmir. At the same time, the sculpture is more primal than in other parts of India, its ornateness contrasted by occasional rough-hewn figures that seem to be less stylized than the rest, asserting a oneness with nature.

Sun worship was prevalent in northern India extending as far south as Gujarat, then known as Saurashtra, till about the 12th century AD. The sun, Surya, also called Martanda, holds a special, if now obscure, place in Hindu mythology. The offspring of Aditi, he is the father of both Manu (man) and Yama (death). As his importance declined in the rest of the country, in Kashmir, which remained cut off and untouched by such changes, the Surya tradition endured.

MARTANDA

Situated on a high plateau, 60 miles south-east of the state capital, Srinagar, and about 3.5 miles east of Anantnag, is Martanda, where three structures devoted to the sun were built. Although some records date them as belonging to the 8th century, according to Kalhana they were erected from 370 to 500 AD, making this arguably the oldest temple site in Kashmir. The sun was worshipped here till the end of the 14th century when its image was destroyed.

At the foot of the plateau is the *tirtha* of Matan (derived from Martanda) or Bavan, where there are some smaller modern temples, sacred springs and tanks worth visiting. A short distance away, at Bumagur, are rare rock-cut caves of some interest to tourists and two temples of note (though the larger of the two, Bhimakeshava, has been converted into a *ziarat* or Islamic pilgrimage centre/shrine).

Surya

The Surya temple, with splendid views of both valley and mountain, is set within a paved court, 220 feet long and 142 feet wide, enclosed by the remains of 83 odd cell-like enclosures. These chapels have trefoiled or three-arched doors resembling a clover leaf, surmounted by triangular pediments. They were arranged 25 each on the northern and southern sides, 19 on the eastern and only 14 on the western boundary. The northern row of cells, in a severe state of ruin, appears like some ancient Greek temple with its classical pillars rising up to support the sky, and large urns can be seen embedded in the ground nearby.

Entering a large porch from the direction of the sunrise, one would come upon the temple constructed from huge blocks of stone, horizontally arranged, with two wings, and as many main apartments — the spacious *naos* (hall) and the oblong *cella* (sanctum) — supported by vaguely Doric pillars. Myths abound about the temple. According to one, Martanda had a wooden roof with 'gilt copper sheets', but this is not likely as stone roof tiles have been found on the grounds.

The lack of any roofs whatsoever today at Martanda emphasizes the feeling of loneliness about the isolated shrine, whose walls are crumbling and whose images lie scattered about the estate, hidden by debris, submerged in pools of water or just broken and piled up on the ground. Once these very same walls must have resounded with the chanting of holy verses, the ringing of bells and these spaces been filled with the fragrance of *pooja* flowers, burning incense and camphor sticks.

The statues of *apsara*-s, *gandharva*-s, and subsidiary gods and goddesses would have stood in place, adding to the sense of exaltation the devotee experienced as he entered the shrine of the sun. Where today the visitor can spy only rock and snow, temple life must have hummed, in miniature imitation of the life in the city, with its vineyards, outside.

The high, arched doorways resemble those of a great church and the blank blocks of stone lend a sense of great age to the structure, which many other temples across India lack due to the very liveliness of their façades. One of the remarkable features of the shrine is a relief on an inner wall of the *antarala* (vestibule). It depicts the Ganga flowing down to the earth for the first time. The river gushes down the Himalayas mischievously and with mighty force, only to be stopped short by Lord Siva, who traps and controls her in his matted hair. Though obviously defaced by marauding hands, this panel is a study in realism. Water 'courses' down the stone in what is an exquisite and rare example of the minor but well developed tradition of sculpture in ancient Kashmir.

Even in decay, Martanda exudes a sense of pomp and circumstance as it lifts its arms up to the first rays of the rising sun.

PANDRETHAN

The site of the ancient city Srinagari, founded by King Asoka in the 3rd century BC, came to be known as Puranadhisthana or the abbreviated Pandrethan, after the capital was shifted to its present location at the end of the 6th century AD. Approximately 50 years before this move, the city had witnessed a great boom in building but the Siva temple and other construction in the vicinity was disfigured in the 14th century by Sultan Sikander, infamous destroyer of many temples in Kashmir.

The Siva shrine of Pandrethan stands on the banks of the Jhelum river, minuscule against the glory of the Himalayan ridges rising up behind it. It is within the present city limits of the Srinagar cantonment, about 3.5 miles outside the city proper, on the Srinagar-Anantnag highway.

The shrine, made of dressed stone, now stands immersed in a pool of water but was originally constructed on a high, *tri ratha* (triangular) platform like the one seen beneath the sanctum sanctorum at Martanda. The style of construction would almost lead one to believe that the temple was made of wood, not stone. It resembles a tiny wooden cottage, with two tiered, tiled roof, dormer windows (in the *chaitya* style) and deep eaves. Pandrethan is far more understated than the archetypal Hindu temple of the Gangetic plains whose ornate carvings and *shikhara* rising high into the sky signal its presence to devotees.

Built between 906 and 921 AD, Pandrethan appears similar to Western classical structures in design and treatment but is the best extant example of the Kashmir style. Its sanctum is square in shape, according to the specific dictates of Hindu architectural tradition, unlike its *tri ratha* arrangement on the outside. The members that hold up the walls are in turn supported by carved elephants. The stark simplicity of the innermost shrine contrasts with the almost embroidery-like intricacy of the pattern on the nine slabbed ceiling above it. The ceiling is created by the 'laying of diagonal and square stone courses to produce designs with rotating and diminishing squares.'[1]

The visually receding pattern is completed by central embellishment — the symbolic lotus spilling over from above. Used all over India, throughout the ages, in various parts of a temple, the lotus was preferred for ceiling decoration. It is surrounded by two rows of very Western-looking cherubs, the single ones with lit lamps, the pairs holding drapery or garlands. Hence the ceiling is an odd mixture of Hindu symbolism and Gothic decoration.

With hardly any evidence, in terms of icons, remaining in the shrine, 19th and early 20th century explorers could only

Built on the typical *tri ratha* embellished platform of the region, there were two auxiliary temples on the plot, constructed at the north-eastern and north-western corners of the court. The whole complex must have been gigantic and breath-taking. Sadly, neither structure nor ornamentation remain in a condition to be much appreciated. Only a statue of Lakulisa, this time standing, supports a niche above the entrance. Faintly discernible is a tableau of Avantivarman and his queen dressed austerely in readiness to pray to Siva.

BADRINATH

Siva, as we know, is not the only god who resides in the Himalayas. Vishnu, the preserving element in the holy trinity, abides there too, beyond the Vale of Flowers. Where Man and God have their meeting place is the shrine of Vishnu on the left bank of the Alakananda river at the holy *tirtha* of Badrinath. This northern centre of pilgrimage is regarded by some to be one of the four holiest places in the country. The others are Dwaraka in the west, Jagannath Puri in the east, and Rameshwaram in the south. Many devout Hindus would not consider a pilgrimage complete unless Badrinath was on the itinerary.

Called a 'supreme place of pilgrimage', Badrinath is almost 180 miles north-east of Rishikesh. It is situated at a height of 10,000 feet above sea level, between two hills, the Nar Parvat (Mountain of Man), and the Narayan Parvat (Mountain of God), where the mortal and the immortal did penance. The *tirtha sthana*, where many sacred texts were said to have been written, apparently existed as early as the 6th century BC. Indeed, legend has it that its Vishnu temple was destroyed some 1,200 years ago.

The present shrine dates back to the 7th century AD. The famous south Indian philosopher Swami Shankaracharya, trekked up to Badrinath with his disciple, Padmapadacharya, and eventually established a *math* (centre of learning) there. He had come to meet and talk with the renowned author of the *Vedanta Sutra*, Badrayan, upon whose work he had written a *bhasya* (commentary).

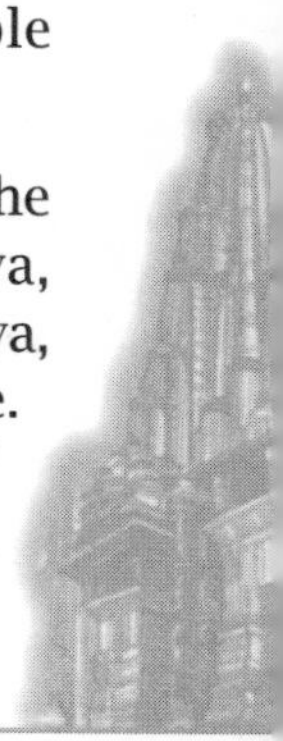

One night, as the learned man slept, Vishnu appeared to him in the form of Sri Narayan, whose idol had been installed at Badrinath centuries ago. The image, which had been thrown long ago into the Narad Kund in the Alakananda, begged Shankaracharya to rescue him and rebuild his temple. This work the hermit delegated to Padampadacharya, who carried out his wishes.

Badrinath is full of shrines and auxiliary structures, the town's life being geared only towards catering to the droves of pilgrims who flock there each year from mid-April to the end of October. It is a place worth visiting more for its natural splendours and the atmosphere of devotion and sanctity rather than its architectural wonders. Five miles away, as the crow flies, is the breathtaking Nilkantha temple. Not constructed by any man, it is an optical illusion and one that must be seen to be believed. The 'temple' is actually the pyramidal peak of the 21,650 foot Nilkantha mountain.

Amarnath

Another natural temple in the region is the Amarnath cave temple, near Mount Kailash.[3] The entrance to this well-known pilgrimage site, located at a height of 13,120 feet, is blocked much of the year. In the rainy season when the snow has thawed, then devout and hardy devotees worship at the place where it is believed Siva shared with Parvati the secrets of immortality.

Pilgrims have been trekking here since before the 12th century when Kalhana recorded the fact in his *Rajtarangini*. In this snowy shrine, large icicles weld together to form a magnificent and glittering Siva linga. In comparison with these natural offerings to God, the 50 foot high shrine at Badrinath is rather unimpressive. The Buddhist influence on its construction is evident; this is only natural considering that when it was built, Buddhism was at its peak and its architectural style had spread far and wide, being absorbed into Hindu construction. However, the garish new paint takes away from any original architectural beauty the building may have possessed. The entrance to the Badrinarayan temple is through a tall arch in the middle of an oddly Indo-Saracenic façade.

Kedarnath ~ Threshold of Eternity

Kedarnath ~ Threshold of Eternity

Fronting the temple is a hot sulphur spring, the Taptapani (boiling water), where the God of fire, Agni resides. Just below this marvel of nature flows the freezing Alakananda. Within the temple complex is the *garba grha* where the idol of the meditating Badrinarayan is placed, adorned with jewels and a diamond on his forehead. The image is shaded by a golden canopy. Nearby is a subsidiary shrine to his consort, Lakshmi, the goddess of wealth and good fortune. There is also a *bhog mandir* (hall of offering), on the estate where rice is cooked as part of the daily care-taking ritual for the god.

KEDARNATH

Not far from Badrinath is another holy *tirtha* where, it is said, 'one finds oneself almost at the threshold of eternity'.[4] This is Kedarnath, with its stark and austere 8th century temple devoted to a mendicant god, Siva. It is built, defying almost every law of construction, below Mahapatha mountain, on a ridge that juts out at right angles to the peak.

Kedarnath has been renowned since time immemorial as hallowed ground. When the heroes of the *Mahabharata*, the *Pandava*-s were wending their way through the Himalayas on their last journey in life, they stopped at this spot. Here the five brothers rested, meditated and prayed to Siva. And here, the youngest of them, Sahadeva, passed away.

At a height of 11,753 feet, Kedarnath is strongly reminiscent of the Tibetan monasteries that are not so far away. Built of dressed stone, it is unembellished by traditional Indian temple sculpture. The entrance to the temple is, like Badrinath, inexplicably Islamic in character but here the blankness of the stonework is relieved by a moulded archway, flanked by pilastered niches meant for the images of attendant gods or *dwarapala*-s (doorkeepers). The *mandapa* possesses a sloping roof as does the sanctum. Its *shikhara* rises up from behind the hall, to meet a golden *amrit ghata* (pot of holy nectar).

The temple remains closed, per force, during the winter. The journey up to the shrine is full enough of hardships even when there is no snow on the ground. Devotees therefore travel to Ukhimath between November and April to worship the image of Kedarnath there.

The northern regions of India are dotted with innumerable pilgrimage centres but the one that probably ranks as high as Badrinath or Kedarnath is Vaishnodevi.[5] Located en route from Jammu to Srinagar, the temple is yet another of Kashmir's natural shrines. Devoted to three mother goddesses, it is visited yearly by pilgrims who climb seven miles to reach it.

Notes

1 *The Hindu Temple - An Introduction to its Meaning and Form*, George Michell, Icon Editions, Harper and Row Publications, 1977, Great Britain

2 *Pandrethan, Avantipur and Martand*, Debala Mitra, Archaeological Survey Of India, New Delhi, 1977

3 *The Call of Badrinath*, Govind Prasad Nautiyal, Second Impression, 1950, The Fine Press, Lucknow

4 *ibid.*

5 *ibid.*

The Kandariya Mahadev ~ Khajuraho

Then even nothingness was not, nor existence.
There was no air then, nor the heavens beyond it.
Who covered it? Where was it? In whose keeping?
Was there then cosmic water, in depths unfathomed?
But, after all, who knows, and who can say,
Whence it all came, and how creation happened?
The gods themselves are later than creation,
So who knows truly whence it has arisen?

Rig-Veda
x, 129

The Kandariya Mahadev - Khajuraho

Then even nothingness was not, nor existence.
There was no air then, nor the heavens beyond it.
Who covered it? Where was it? In whose keeping?
Was there then cosmic water, in depths unfathomed?
But, after all, who knows, and who can say,
Whence it all came, and how creation happened?
The gods themselves are later than creation,
So who knows truly whence it has arisen?

Rig-Veda
x, 129

Where It All Began

The Temples of Central India

Khajuraho — Kandariya Mahadev, Lakshmana, Chausat Yogini, Matangeshwara, Duladeo; **Varanasi** — Viswanatha, Durga; **Gaya, Ayodhya, Mathura, Vrundavan, Hardwar, Gwalior** — Teli Ka Mandir, Sas-Bahu; **Gyraspur** — MalaDevi; **Udayapur**— Neelkanteshwar

The architectural style loosely termed Nagara or metropolitan, refers to a wide range of temples built over a large expanse of time and space across the trunk of the Indian subcontinent. This stretches from Uttar Pradesh in the north to Maharashtra in the south and from Rajasthan in the west to the borders of Bengal in the east. It encompasses much of Uttar Pradesh, Haryana, Madhya Pradesh and Bihar.

The region, broadly known as central India, home of the Ganga and the Yamuna rivers, flowing down from the Himalayas, was well-watered and fertile. This was one of the reasons why not only civilization could take birth and prosper here but the seeds of Hinduism could germinate and blossom. It was also, almost continuously, the core around which empires flourished, the premier one being the Mauryan in the 3rd and 4th centuries BC.

When its ruler, the famous Asoka; newly converted to Buddhism, advocated the use of stone for building, it was a crucial turning point in the history of Indian architecture. Prior to this era, builders used materials like timber, plaster, and brick, which explains why hardly any pre-Mauryan structures survive in India today. The next major impetus to the art of construction came from the Guptas (400-600 AD), who re-advocated the use of stone but on a larger scale and over a wider area. Although not many of their flat-roofed shrines survive (most extant examples are located in this prosperous Gangetic basin), they set a trend for construction that would lead to the evolution of the temple form.

The central province is a mini-representation of the entire nation with its varying climates, geography, races, cultures and religions. Little wonder then that its Hindu building tradition is complex and varied. The style of religious architecture, Hindu, Buddhist, and Jaina, that has developed in central India over the past 2,000 years and more, contains some of the most diverse and rich temples in the country. It outlines the evolution of the art from its earliest extant brick temple at Bhitargaon, to the pioneering Gupta rock edicts, pillars, and cave *chaitya*-s at Sanchi and Bodhgaya; from the highly developed tradition of Khajuraho and beyond to the later post-Mughal structures built by Hindu princes in Varanasi and Vrundavan.

In the history of northern Hindu architecture, the regions that stand out as excellent examples of the Nagara (also called Indo-Aryan) style, are Rajasthan-Gujarat; Orissa; and Central India. Within this last are the renowned temples at Khajuraho, in the Bundelkhand district of Madhya Pradesh. The three groups of temples at Khajuraho, famous foremost for their erotic sculptures which draw tourists from all over the world, in reality are the acme of expertise and refinement reached by medieval Nagara architects, after the rules and guidelines for construction had been evolved by their classical predecessors.

Khajuraho

Khajuraho is divine in the real sense of the word. Not because it is a city of temples, unequalled in elegance, intricacy, and beauty but because it was built by the Chandela dynasty, whose founder is thought to have belonged to the family of Sribrahmandmuni or Brahma, the holy creator of the universe.

The acclaimed Arab traveller of the 14th century, Ibn Batuta, recorded a fantastic description of Khajuraho in his memoirs. He saw the great capital of the Chandelas in 1335 AD, when he visited it during the reign of Mahmud Shah Tuglaq. 'There is a lake', said Batuta, at what he called Kajura, 'about a mile in length, and around this lake are temples in which there are idols. At this place reside a tribe of *jogi*-s (mendicants) with long and matted hair. Their colour is yellow, which arises from their fasting. Many of the Muslims of these parts attend on them and learn magic from them'.

The earliest mention of the city, variously called Sri Khajuravahaka, Khajurapura and Khajjinpura, comes from Abu Rihan, who accompanied the invader, Mahmud of Ghazni to India in 1022 AD, and mentioned it as the capital of the kingdom of Jijoti. Whether this was true or not is unknown. However, Khajuraho certainly was large, as its ruins, covering eight square miles, show.

According to legend, the main gateway to the town was ornamented with two golden palm trees, hence its name, 'the place of the date palm'. More likely, it derives from the preponderance of palm trees in the locality. A great annual fair was held here on the occasion of *Mahasivaratri*, the birthday of Lord Siva. The fair is one tradition that has apparently survived to the present time though very few pilgrims attend it now.

The theory that a city once existed here makes a little more understandable the mystery of why the Chandelas, staunch Saivites, created a fabulous array of intricate and erotic Saiva, Vaishnava and Jaina temples in an otherwise unattractive location, absolutely off the beaten track. Where did the artisans come from? Who were their models? How was such a large-scale project financed? Few clues remain.

Today Khajuraho is but a sleepy little town of some 6,000 people, 27 miles from Chhatarpur, situated at the south-eastern corner of the Khajuraho Sagar or Nimora Tal that

Ibn Batuta wrote about. At the lake, only about 20 structures survive, from the 85 that supposedly once existed. Although many fell prey to time and lack of maintenance, Sultan Sikander Lodi is responsible for the destruction of the others in 1494-1495, only 500 years after their construction.

The temples, all built in the Indo-Aryan style between 950 and 1050 AD, indicate a continuous spate of activity in an already finely honed art rather than a stage of an evolutionary process. They are arranged in three groups; the western, eastern and southern, all but one being oriented north to south. The structures are externally very similar, built in granite or a combination of light coloured sandstone (imported from the Panna quarries) and granite. Since many of the idols of the main deities have been removed or defaced, it is often puzzling to distinguish which deity a temple was dedicated to.

In the hot, dusty and bare landscape, Khajuraho emerges as an oasis. The shrines are distinctive in their elevation, most of them consisting of a series of joint structures rising up like mountain ridges, one after another, the lowermost point being the porch and the highest the sanctum. The gradual incline leads the eye up from the gateway to the *mandapa* roofs and the building's *shikhara*, offering up, in a sense, the devotee's soul to god. This exalting element is enhanced by the raising of these structures on high platforms rather as a precious stone would be set in a ring to display it to the best advantage.

Most of the locality's temples have the ground plan of a cross with only one entrance from the east. In true Nagara fashion, they all possess a *garba grha* surrounded by the *pradakshina* path. The sanctuary is entered through an *antarala* which follows a large *mahamandapa* (grand or main hall). Variations to this plan occur in the form of an entrance porch or *ardhmandapa* (half hall) and a *mandapa* intended for dancing or offering being sometimes added, much like the temples of Orissa. Some Khajuraho temples are *panchayatana,* with a special shrine devoted to the vehicle of the chief god.

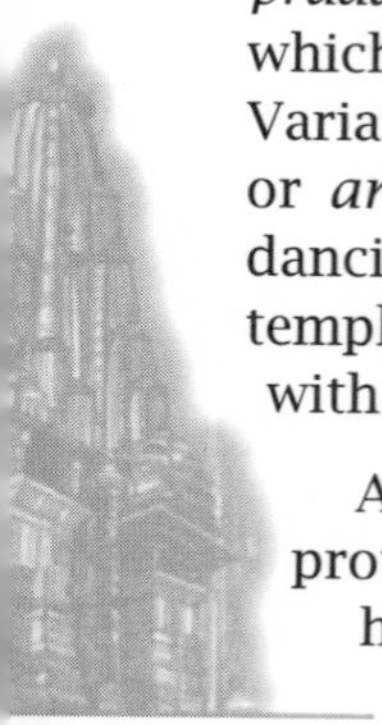

A striking feature of the structures is their *oriel* window, protruding out from the main structure like a balcony, and heavily carved. It provides light and air to the *pradakshina*

path and *mahamandapa*. Horizontal against the verticality of the *shikhara*, it casts deep shadows across the carvings. It also resembles very much the palace windows of Rajasthan. A Rajput princess appearing at such a balcony might be quite apropos.

The decoration covering every part of the temple exterior, and much of the interior, is as deliberate as the building's plan. No flourish is an afterthought, every story depicted is essential to the desired design effect. The purpose at Khajuraho almost seems to have been for sculptors to record contemporary life for the benefit of future generations. Although there are bizarre theories for the existence of the detailed sexual carvings here, documentation of a way of life is perhaps the best explanation, the generations who built these temples probably being unfettered by the inhibitions that came to bind Indian society centuries later.

Western Group

Kandariya Mahadeva

The western group of temples, Saiva and Vaishnava in faith, is the best preserved at Khajuraho and is arranged in two rows. Each contains one large temple followed by smaller ones. The biggest, most lavish, and best known is the reddish-white Kandariya Mahadeva that has graced the covers of countless books on Indian temples. The proportions of Kandariya Mahadeva are impressive enough in themselves — the shrine is 102 feet long, 67 feet wide, with a tower 118 feet high. When the best possible planning and craftsmanship are added to this, small wonder that it is representative of this sophisticated group.

Dedicated to Siva, the *panchayatana* shrine was built between 1025 and 1050 AD. Today, only the main structure remains out of its original five. All were constructed on a high platform, though, of course, the subsidiary ones were much smaller in size and visually connected by long stone benches where pilgrims could rest a while.

The plinth, reached by a high flight of stairs, was moulded, with nine, evenly spaced niches for the statues of Siva, Ganesha and the seven mother goddesses, *matrika*-s (or *sakti*-s). *Sakti*

also means female energy, the principle of life (see Kamaksha temple, Chapter 5). Ingeniously planned, the platform also projects out at the cardinal points, to match the oriel windows above. These exquisite balconies allow in just enough light to make visible the sculptures in the *garba grha.*

One enters the extravagantly worked, rectangular portico and nave through a graceful carved *torana*, as if it were ivory, with figures of gorgons, *gandharva*-s, and *deva*-s. The interior of the temple is as painstakingly carved as the outer areas. The chambers are elevated, as it were, by the airy and light, receding carvings on their coffered ceiling. In detail, they greatly resemble the fabulous marble Jaina temples of Mount Abu.

The *garba grha* is also adorned at its entrance with carvings. Here ascetics meditate, the river goddesses guard the lord of the mountains and stone flowers offer themselves to god. Framed by this richness is *Shankara* (Siva) as a marble *linga.* His abode is, as his Himalayan cave, dark and free of embellishment. In the peace and shade, the god rests, soothing worshippers by his silent, strong presence.

Around the sanctum runs the decorated *pradakshina* path, its moulded plinth bearing figures of the *ashtadikpala*-s (eight guardian gods) — Indra, Agni, Yama, Nairita, Varuna, Vayu, Kubera and Isana — who guard Siva. Above these, set in the wall, are recesses for statues of each member of the holy trinity.

The three horizontal bands of sculpture on the walls are indented in places, projecting out in others, creating a sense of undulation throughout the building and heightening some sculptures with light while concealing others by the consequent shade. On a hot day, the building shimmers like a mirage.

The multitude of *deva*-s, *devi*-s (goddesses) and voluptuous *apsara*-s — according to one account, 872 in all — on the walls, appear as lovers, dreamers and warriors. All the human and divine figures seem entranced, as if filled with an inner joy. Their eyes look beyond the viewer into some private heaven of their own. Even in the erotic sculptures, the ecstasy on the couples' faces is more divine than earthly. Obviously, the creators of Khajuraho were not only highly skilled, trained, and deeply religious, but also well-versed in the *Kama Sutra.*

The external decoration also includes rows of reliefs over which lines of molding are carved. Beyond further bands of sculpture, miniature towers meet the central one. Above the temple which eloquently expresses both worldly and spiritual desires, the main *shikhara* of Kandariya Mahadeva rises up in a parabolic curve, in imitation of the joined hands of a pilgrim doing a *namaskar* (attitude of prayer).

LAKSHMANA

The Lakshmana ji ka mandir is, funnily enough, not dedicated to Rama's brother of the same name. But how this shrine got its name is unclear as it is undoubtedly Vishnu's. It is known for the superior quality of its reliefs and an unusual shrine with its carving of a *guru* (teacher) and his *sisya*-s (students).

Although similar in design to its neighbour, the Kandariya Mahadeva, the Lakshmana is smaller in scale yet appears more spread-out in elevation than the sharply rising Kandariya. Ninety-eight feet long and 45 feet wide, it has five bays, traditional oriel windows, and an exquisitely carved, cusped *torana.*

The exterior of the shrine displays various *sthambha*-s or positions from the *Kama Sutra* and continues the Kandariya's process of documenting Khajuraho life in scenes of wrestling matches, devotional groups, dances, elephant fights and the like. Inside, the lintel above the sanctum entrance is carved with figures of Brahma, rarely seen in Indian temples, and Lakshmi, flanked by two small altars. Further above this is a representation of the cosmos with the *nava graha*-s (nine planets). The carved door jambs present tableaux of the story of the churning of the ocean by the *devas* and the demons, as well as the incarnations of Vishnu. The sanctum's image, framed in a *torana,* is of a four foot high, three-armed, four-headed Vishnu. The central head is human while the other two represent his incarnations of Narasimha, the man-lion, and Varaha, the boar.

Compared to other temple sculptures, the story-telling element of those at Lakshmana is fascinating. Not only is the work unusual, but some of the tales it tells are uncommon. The relief of Revanta is an example. The sun god, Surya, is depicted all across India in temples either devoted to him or as a subsidiary god. But this rare relief of Surya's son, Revanta, on a horse, out for the day, boar hunting, brings a lesser known mythological character to life, placing him in the social context of the day.

Chausat Yogini

The 64 *yogini*-s (priestesses) who give this temple its name, are the attendants of Kali (or Durga) and were housed in an unusual temple open to the sky. It was built in 900 AD and is situated on a rocky ledge east of the Shiv Sagar or 'lake of Siva'.

This place of worship, perhaps belonging to a Tantric cult, is unlike the rest of the Khajuraho structures. It is formed of 65 cells, topped by small *shikhara*-s and *chaitya*-style windows, on the periphery of an oblong courtyard. Today, only 35 are standing. All but one are the same size and were meant to hold images of *yogini-s*. They probably had wooden doors to protect the idols. The larger altar in the middle of the south-western wall faces the entrance and was, according to some sources, intended for the image of Kali. Others claim it for Siva Bhairava. There are currently three deities placed in it, one of Mahishasuramardini (another name for Kali, who killed the demon Mahishasura), and two retrieved from the subsidiary shrines and representing the mother goddesses, Brahmani and Maheshwari.

Mtangeshvara

The only live Hindu temple of Khajuraho, Matangeshwara is sacred to the royal family of the area and the other inhabitants. The east-facing temple, studded with oriel windows, stands close to the Lakshmana. Its unique feature is the large *yoni* (the female symbol — the counterpart of the *linga* or phallic symbol), four feet high, set in the floor of its *garba grha*. Twenty feet in diameter, it holds a highly polished *linga*, eight feet tall and three feet wide.

Eastern Group

The Eastern group of Khajuraho temples consists mostly of the Jaina shrines — the Parsvanatha, Adinatha, Shanti Natha, and Ghantai — built by the religiously tolerant Chandelas. There is also a collection of minor Hindu temples like the Javari, Vamana, Brahma and Hanuman. Of these, the first three are devoted to Vishnu, the Vamana being dedicated to his dwarf incarnation, and the sandstone and granite Brahma temple, one of the oldest at Khajuraho, being erroneously named.

Hanuman, the monkey god and faithful aide of Rama, was once widely worshipped in north India (he is still highly revered in the state of Maharashtra). The Hanuman temple contains an eight foot depiction of him, dated 922 AD.

Southern Group

Only two temples remain of this southern group — the Chaturbhuj and the Duladeo, the former housing a massive image of Vishnu, the latter probably the last shrine to be built here.

The Duladeo is a Siva shrine but the name means the 'Holy Bridegroom'. The story goes that a bridal procession was passing the temple when the groom died at its door and turned into a god. The small, graceful, five-chambered temple possesses some of the famous Khajuraho erotic carvings but it is felt to be not as well constructed as its predecessors.

Varanasi

I come to you as a child to his mother.
I come as an orphan to you, moist with love.
I come without refuge to you, giver of sacred rest.
I come a fallen man to you, uplifter of all.
I come undone by disease to you, the perfect physician.
I come, my heart dry with thirst, to you, ocean of sweet wine.
Do with me whatever you will."

Jagannatha - Gangalahari (17th century)

Pious Hindus go to the eternal city to breathe their last for they believe that dying in the holy *kshetra* of Varanasi, on the banks of the river Ganga, ensures for them a passage to heaven. This seems appropriate when one considers how often this city has 'died' but been reborn as sacred.

The temples of Varanasi have been razed to the ground repeatedly in its long and colourful history. Indeed, it is ironic and unfortunate that this temple town, whose shrines have been mentioned in ancient texts like the *Purana-s*, should today possess 1,500 temples, yet not one which can definitely be attributed to the pre-Mughal period.

The lack of such ancient religious architecture has not reduced the fame of Varanasi nor lessened the fervour of its people. This ancient but ageless, crowded yet calm, noisy but serene place, is a *tirtha* for both Hindus and Jainas and an acclaimed centre of learning even in this century. The holy spirit of the town called Avimnktakshetra, Mahasmasana, Andavana and most recently Benares, is immortal.

The ancient kingdom, Kashi, of which Benares was the capital, also gave its name to the city. However, it is now known by the two rivers that border it, the Varuna and the Asi — Varanasi. This city of *ghat*-s (steps or a landing on a river) is unique, for here the Ganga, which has a south-eastern course, inexplicably turns northward.

The city's patron god was Vishveshwar, Lord of the World. His shrine, the Visvanatha, existed at least as far back as the 7th century, for when the Chinese traveller Huen Tsang, came to the city, he called it 'an imposing structure with a spire of about 100 feet in height'.

Kutb-uddin Aibak[1] supposedly razed about 100 temples in Varanasi in 1194 AD. Allaud-din Khilji[2] and Ibrahim Lodhi[3] followed suit. After the 1669 demolition of the Visvanatha temple, its sacred *linga* was kept hidden by the priests. When it was finally brought out for worship, it was moved from site to site until *Gokulashtami* day in 1777 AD, when the shrine ordered by the Maratha Maharani of Indore, Rani Ahilya Bai Holkar, a temple saviour of sorts, was complete.

The Visvanatha temple is small, with a sanctum only 10 square feet in area, its spire a mere 30 feet high. Its gilt covering was donated by Raja Ranjit Singh of the Punjab some years later. On the same estate is the Gyan Vapi mosque on the site where the original shrine had been.

Hardwar ~ Gateway to God

The building incorporated the walls of the older structure but part of its *mandapa* is still visible.

Benares, which had traditionally been one of the abodes of Siva, is replete with lore about the dark-skinned god. One tale recounts how one day Siva threw his mighty *trishul* (trident) to the ground and water spurted forth. The well of the Visvanatha temple is said to have been dug on that holy spot.

Of the hundreds of temples in Varanasi, the most famous are the Kalabhairava, Annapurna, Sakshi-Vinayaka, the Bindu Madhava, and the temple of the monkeys. The first of these belongs to the guardian of the city and was located in the same compound as the Visvanatha in the 16th century. Today, it is in an altogether different part of the city, though the Annapurna and Sakshi Vinayaka are just a walk away.

The temple of the monkeys is, in reality, a shrine to Durga. The warrior goddess has been worshipped in the city since the 6th century AD. Once, when she laid down her sword, it is said the impression it made on the earth created the Asi river. An 11th century shrine to her was located near the Durga Kund, 100 yards from the same river. But the shrine that today stands there, was built by Rani Bhavani Bai of Natore, in the 18th century AD.

The pilgrim going to Varanasi encounters a packed town with narrow streets and shrines at every turn. He is 'expected to visit daily the Visvanatha, Bindu Madhava, Dhundi Raja and Durga temples' and take a dip at any one of the *ghat*-s, most built by Maratha rulers or generals, along the Ganga. Of these, the most sacred are the Dasashvamedha, Panchganga and Manikarnika, where at dawn pilgrims are seen bathing in the now-filthy waters upon which float remnants of the previous day's *pooja* — flowers, leaves and fruit offered up to god — as the skyline of the city glows into sunrise.

GAYA, AYODHYA, MATHURA, VRUNDAVAN, HARDWAR

Not far from Kashi, are two sacred sites in Bihar — Bodhgaya of the Buddhists and Gaya of the Hindus. The former is worshipped as the site where Gautama Buddha received enlightenment, the latter is a *tirtha* with special purifying powers for sinners. Here pilgrims come to lay the restless spirits of ancestors to rest and to see the extraordinary foot of Vishnu, imprinted in solid rock and measuring 40 centimeters in length (see also Vishnupaad temple, Pandharpur, Chapter 7). It is worshipped at Gaya's *Vishnupad* (Vishnu's foot) temple, built in 1787, under the patronage of the generous temple-building queen, Ahilya Bai. She was responsible for the construction of scores of shrines, like those at Varanasi and Pandharpur, across India.

Other highly revered *tirtha sthana*-s in India's central basin include Ayodhya, the birthplace of Rama, with over 1,000 temples and now the site of sectarian controversy; the whole region around Mathura where Krishna was born about 3,500 years ago; and Vrundavan (in Uttar Pradesh), the picturesque forest of *tulsi* or sacred basil where he cavorted with his playmates. The *tulsi* plant is revered by the Hindus and the town of Vrundavan gives its name to the basil stand found in the centre of the courtyard of traditional Hindu homes.

Mathura was renowned in ancient records as an important Buddhist centre of learning but is today visited by Krishna devotees for its associations with the god — the prison cell where he was born (now located in the Keshava Deo temple), the Potara tank where his nappies were washed and the Vishram (rest or repose) Ghat where he relaxed after killing his evil uncle, King Kansa.

In Vrundavan, there are over 4,000 temples of varying antiquity, and probably even more widows, for they come here after the death of their husbands to escape brutality or indifference at the hands of relatives. They inhabit the town's many *dharamshala*-s, spending the rest of their lives shorn of hair and dressed in austere white, singing the praises of the divine prankster, Govind.

Govind is one of Krishna's infinite names. Each signifies a particular aspect about him, his colouring, his playful nature, his exploits as a lover, his pursuits, his wisdom. Some of these names are Shyam, Hari (also used to refer to God in general), Shridhar, Vanmali, Keshava, Madhava, Gopal, Giridhar, Mukund, and Govardhan.

Located further north is the temple town of Hardwar, called the Gateway or Door (*Dwar*) to God (*Hari*), because of its proximity to the Himalayas, where the gods lived. It is also one of the four sacred spots in India where the nectar of immortality fell from the *kumbha* (pot) of the gods. The others are Allahabad, Ujjain and Nasik. At these sites, the Kumbha Mela, a pilgrimage-festival, is held every three years.

GWALIOR

The royal city of Gwalior in Madya Pradesh, famous for its fort and its Teli ka Mandir (the oilman's temple), is named after the hermit Gwalipa. Local lore has it that Gwalipa lived where the hill fort now stands. The legendary founder of the city, Prince Suraj Sen, suffered from leprosy. Gwalipa apparently cured him of it by giving him miraculous water to drink from a tank, now called Suraj Kund, outside his hut. He also gave the prince a new name, Suhan Pal, and told him that as long as his descendants used that surname, they would remain in power.

Suhan Pal built the fort at the site of his healing and different dynasties ruled it over the centuries. Of historic note is the fact that the brave Rani Lakshmi Bai, queen of the neighbouring principality of Jhansi, who opposed British rule in India, fought her last battle and was killed here.

Gwalior Fort houses not only the restored Teli Ka Mandir but also several large rock-cut Jaina carvings, two reservoirs, the Sas-Bahu Mandir, and the Chaturbhuj shrine. This last is the earliest surviving temple in the fort. Dedicated to Vishnu, the temple of the four-armed god was hewn out of the rockface in 876 AD, but is important more as a historic monument than an architectural one.

The 9th century Teli Ka Mandir is the oldest surviving work of the Pratihara dynasty (8th to 10th century AD) and is therefore of considerable import. Resembling in character the Portuguese cathedrals of Bassein (an old settlement near Bombay, Maharashtra), it is an unusual structure combining consciously or unconsciously both the Dravida and Nagara styles of architecture. At a staggering height of 1,000 feet, it appears squat due to its wagon or barrel shaped *shikhara* resembling a *gopuram* (a Dravida temple's towered gateway) or a vaulted church ceiling.

Nonetheless, all its plentiful decorative detail is north Indian in origin. On either side of its round top, beneath which fits a horseshoe window, the shrine has sloping roofs, another uncommon feature in the region. It is unique in appearance and perhaps, therefore, fails to evoke the sense of solemnity that other temples do easily.

The Sas-Bahu Mandir actually consists of two temples, one larger than the other. This difference in size gives the two their shared name of 'The Shrine of the Mother-in-law and Daughter-in-law', drawing on the well-known unequal relationship that these women traditionally hold in Indian society or indeed, anywhere in the world.

Situated at a scenic site on the eastern side of Gwalior Fort, overlooking the city on the plains, these otherwise twin shrines were started by Padmapala, a Kachhawaha Rajput prince and completed by his successor and brother, Mahipala, in 1093 AD. Commonly held to be Jaina structures, they are in actuality, dedicated to Vishnu and are worth seeing for their ornate door, ceiling and pillar decorations.

GYRASPUR

The cruciform temple of Mala Devi at Gyraspur, a small town 30 miles north of Sanchi, Madhya Pradesh, belongs to a collection of structures — fort, temples and tanks — erected by the builder kings of western India, the Pratiharas. Constructed between the 9th and 10th centuries AD, Mala Devi is a precursor to the forts of Rajputana (as Rajasthan was formerly known), with its balconies and windows, elevated location and intricate carving of religious motifs across its exterior. Its curving *shikhara* is topped by a sculpted *amalaka* (dome or crown), and it possesses in addition to its sanctum, a *pradakshina* path, vestibule and covered *mandapa.*

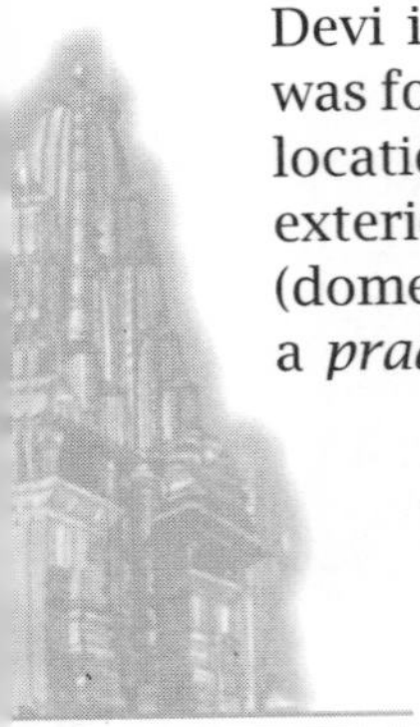

Teli ka Mandir ~ Oilman's Temple

Teli ka Mandir ~ Oilman's Temple

UDAYAPUR

The Neelkanteshwar shrine at Udayapur, the 'City of the Dawn' (not to be confused with the palace city, Udaipur in Rajasthan) is unique for its planning. Its alignment is such that the Siva *linga* in the *garba grha* catches the first rays of the sun every morning.

Located in a small hamlet, 54 miles north of the great Buddhist *stupa* at Sanchi, is the temple of the Blue Throated Siva, so named to record the feat of the god who, once upon a time, swallowed poison to save the world. The toxic liquid was so powerful that his throat turned blue. The shrine is medieval in style and was built in 1059 AD. Almost, but not quite, excessively decorated with five beautifully carved vertical bands like large beads on its fantastic spire, it looks like an engraving come to life.

Note

1 Kutb-uddin Aibak was the general and viceroy of the 12th century invader, Muhammed of Ghori, who invaded and plundered India.

2 The Turk, Allaud-din Khilji, belonged to the second ruling family of the Muslim Sultanate of Delhi (1290-1320).

3 Ibrahim Lodhi (16th century), was the last Afghan Sultan of the Lodhi dynasty in Delhi.

The Sun Temple ~ Konarak

If the measurement of the temple is in every way perfect,
there will be perfection in the universe as well.

Mayamata
XXII.92

The Sun Temple - Konarak

If the measurement of the temple is in every way perfect,
there will be perfection in the universe as well.

Mayamata
XXII.92

The Land of the Sun

The Temples of the East

Orissa—Lingaraja, Parsurameshwar, Vaitul Deul, Rajarani, Jagannatha, Konark; **Bangal** — Kalighat, Dakshineshwar, Bishnupur, Bansberia; **Assam** — Kamaksha

Orissa

The Kalinga of mixed fortunes was the seat of distinguished dynasties and had a history that spanned over a millennium. King Asoka won a major victory there against the local ruler. According to legend, the sight of the bloodshed he had caused, affected Asoka so deeply that he converted to the peace-promoting religion of Buddhism. He spent the rest of his life doing good deeds rather than conquering territory. Renowned sovereigns notwithstanding, Kalinga is famous all over the world today for its rich collection of religious architecture built between the mid-seventh and 12th centuries AD.

Kalinga, Orissa, or Utkala as it was known in the 10th century, at the pinnacle of its building activity, presents in its three major temple sites the most highly evolved culmination point of centuries of the Nagara tradition. Even the novitiate has heard of the magnificent shrines at the temple towns of Bhubaneshwar and Puri and the Black Pagoda on the seashore at Konark. The existing religious architecture in this region was mostly constructed by the Kesari dynasty and some temples were built by the Gangas who succeeded them. They are elegant of form, intricate of sculpture and possess loftier *shikhara-s* than any others in India. In fact, to create such high spires was the aim of the medieval architects responsible for the construction of this group.

As far as Orissan temple heritage goes, contemporary documentation has yielded sociologically valuable and intriguing facts not only about the processes involved in the financing, planning and construction of temples and the infrastructure needed for such large-scale projects, but also insights into the religious traditions that moulded their architects and guided their work.

While the Orissan temples follow a more or less typical pattern, their distinctiveness comes from individual variation. They were square in plan with a pyramidal roof, and consisted basically of two apartments, the *garba grha* or *deul* as it is called here and the *antarala* (called *jagmohan* or porch in this region). Often additions were made to this outline in the form of one or two *mandapa-s*. Interiors tended to be plain, apart from carved ceiling designs and images in the sanctum sanctorum, but the intricacy and extent of embellishment on the exteriors increased as time went by. The style of sculpture was detailed and enthusiastic but without the florid exaggeration seen in southern India.

The capital of the modern state of Orissa, Bhubaneshwar, possesses some of the oldest architecture in the region. Indeed, it is one of India's foremost temple towns, bustling and dirty, home to hundreds of temples of various ages and crowded with devotees and tourists. It is hard to believe that once upon a time all that had existed here was, perhaps, a thick forest of mango trees.

Siva was discouraged. The holy city of Varanasi was being defiled by infidels and the god felt it was time to leave that temporal abode in search of a new one. So, taking the advice of a wise sage, he chose a dense grove of mango, which happened to be already sacred to Vishnu. Siva had to request the other god for permission to settle there. When he did so, Vishnu agreed but only on the condition that Siva never return to Varanasi. This the god would not agree to until Vishnu reassured him that the new site had every advantage that his old home possessed.

And so it came to be that Vishnu took over as his residence, the *tirtha* of Varanasi while Siva in the form of a *linga* stayed in the Orissan forest. This wood, eons later, grew into the town of Bhubaneshwar (Lord of the World), a sacred city devoted to Siva worship. According to another legend, the city was established by the great ruler, Yayati, founder of the Kesari dynasty, who made Bhubaneshwar a city of 'powerful religions'.

Its sacred pool, the Bindu Sagar, which measures over 1,200 by 650 feet, according to local myth, contains water from every holy water body in the country and was once encircled by 7,000 shrines. Today there are fewer than 500. In the middle of the tank is a small island with a pavilion dedicated to Shankara, where, once a year, his image is immersed in the holy water.

The traveller might be hard put to make a choice among the scores of religious sites worth visiting in the temple town of Bhubaneshwar. The downside of travelling in a many-splendoured country like India is that some places of interest will always be overlooked for lack of time. Certainly the shrines which should not be missed in this city include the great Lingaraja, the smaller Parsurameshwar and Vaitul Deul, the Rajarani, and the Mukteshwar, as well as the brahmanical sandstone caves of the Udayagiri and Khandagiri Hills, located not far from the urban centre.

Lingaraja

King Yayati is also credited with the building of Bhubaneshwar's largest temple, the Lingaraja, situated by the Bindu Sagar and housing the *linga* that Siva is thought to have disappeared into so many eons before. Although widely believed that Yayati was mythical, inscriptions at the Jagannatha temple at Puri indicate that he was real and it was he who ordered the

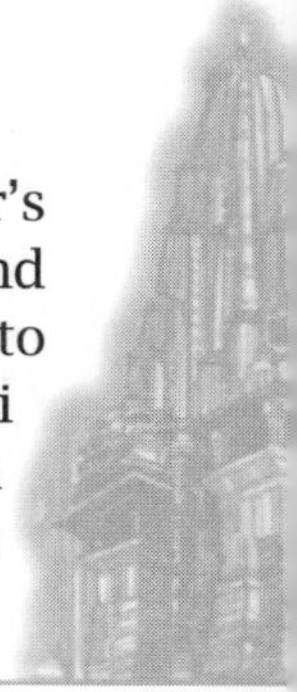

construction of this shrine sacred to the great Lord of the Three Worlds, the Tribhuvaneshwar.

The Lingaraja is a long structure still in use and regrettably open only to Hindus. Enclosed by a high wall, meant to protect it from invaders, it can nevertheless be viewed by others from a platform outside built long ago by the British. The shrine has a remarkable, neatly constructed *vimana* (tower), 127 feet high. An architectural wonder, it consists of several vertical sections, the recesses of which are filled with more miniature *vimana*, all created with painstaking precision. Jutting out in Gothic fashion from its peak, just below the *amalaka*, are a series of lions, the emblem of the Kesari rulers, patrons of the shrine. The spire is hollow, made up of several chambers reached by a stairwell built through the seven inch thick wall. Its height is in sharp contrast to the squatter *mandir* in front of it.

The largest structure, known as the Sri Mandir, placed in a tiled courtyard studded with 65 temples of varying sizes, towers above Bhubaneshwar. It is not only this which catches the eye. The whole group of temples, seeming to surge towards the chief sanctum, tempts the visitor to wander, as in a forest, and brings to mind the conglomeration of Buddhist *stupa-s* at Bodhgaya in Bihar. Many of the small structures are miniatures of the Sri Mandir, probably built by devotees. This arrangement of the shrines, rather like a field of sunflowers turning their faces up to the sun, was built in the early 11th century. However, certain sections of the complex are almost 1,400 years old while some are much more recent.

Climbing a stone staircase to the temple, one enters a series of open pavilions, the first a large *bhog mandir*, square in plan. Beyond this is a smaller section, the dancing hall. Both these porches were added on to the original structure roughly 200 years after it was first built. From the place where the *devadasi*-s[1] (woman 'married' to god who danced in worship of him), must have danced in religious fervour before god, one enters the pillared porch to the *deul*. The interior here is unembellished and austere in atmosphere compared to the fussiness of external detail. The deity is represented by a phallus in the form of a large block of granite. It is set in a *yoni* made of dark chlorite. A Parvati temple in the south-east corner of the Lingaraja compound is attributed to the Ganga dynasty and was probably constructed in the 12th century AD.

Parsurameshwar

Bhubaneshwar's 'Grove of the Perfect Beings' is a grouping of 20 small temples, the oldest and best preserved of which is the Parsurameshwar. It represents some eight shrines of the early Orissa group. The name of this Siva temple actually means 'the Lord of Parasurama', the supreme being as it were, for Parasurama himself was one of Vishnu's incarnations. Built around 750 AD, the shrine exemplifies, with its primitive *vimana* but sophisticated carvings of elephant and horse processions and lattice work, the nascent Orissan architecture of the post-Gupta period.

Parsurameshwar, only 48 feet long, is constructed of stone that ranges in hue from orange and red to purple, colouring the whole structure an unusual shade. Its square sanctum, with a tower 44 feet high but oddly horizontal in character, is disjointed from the flat roofed, rectangular, columned *antarala* in front of it. More like a cell than a porch, its walls are punctuated by unusual 'pierced' stone windows and grilled doorways so thickly decorated with delicately carved figures of dancers and musicians that they scarcely allow any light to enter. Indeed the characters, engaged in beating drums or playing the flute, 'holding up' these entrances as it were, seem to be clustered there to look out interestedly at the approaching devotee. One can almost hear their curious murmurs as one nears the *mandir.*

Vaitual Deul

Vaitul Deul, a Tantric shrine devoted to the worship of Chamundi (as Kali is sometimes called), is situated near the Bindu Sagar, a stone's throw from the mighty Lingaraja temple. It belongs to approximately the same era as the Parsurameshwar, however, the 8th century structure, rectangular in form as specified by traditional architectural treatises, is unique in Bhubaneshwar. The two-storeyed roof, vaulted and wagon-like, with ridged finials and gable ends, seems to derive from the Buddhist *chaitya.* The tower, on the other hand, resembles the Dravidian *Bhima Ratha* of Mahabalipuram in Tamil Nadu, but whether this latter similarity is due to any academic exchange between the two communities or a coincidence is unknown.

Vaitul Deul is probably a very early and unevolved example of the *panchayatana* style of building, for its unusually rectangular *jagmohan* contains, at every corner, a replica of the main shrine. The tower of the small temple rises up only about 35 feet while the ground plan measures 18 by 25 feet.

The rectangular tower is formed by horizontal bands of stone, broken by thin recesses beneath the vaulted roof. Some of the cornices are simply moulded, others ridged for visual relief. At evenly spaced positions across the stonework are carved, miniature horseshoe style windows, complete with face peering out. The sides of the temple have false but heavily decorated entranceways, unreachable because of their distance from the ground, and blocked by *apsara*-s or goddesses, standing in them.

Above the figures, the doorway curves into a traditionally Buddhist arch and is, in fact, crowned by a Buddha-like hermit in meditation. In other recesses distributed across the temple's façade the *apsara*-s reappear, employed in the activities of their boudoirs. Around them, all manner of curlicues curve and flowers bloom with utter disregard to gravity.

One large tableau at the temple depicts an Aryan-faced Surya, with high cheekbones and prominent, straight nose. He is surrounded by a halo created by the glow of the sun. He stands in his famous chariot, driven by the god of the dawn, Uday, the vehicle pulled by seven gigantic horses. These are arranged below the panel ledge and serve not only to 'move' the chariot but to support the sculpture as well. The god appears to be riding into war for he is armed and his attendants are aiming their arrows at an invisible enemy.

The worshipper reaches Vaitul Deul's traditionally dark *garba grha* from the hall by way of a small vestibule, designed to indicate the proximity of his destination and remind him that his attention should now be focused only on prayer. This sanctum sanctorum is a rare change from the norm of the unadorned altar that most Indian temples adhere to. Perhaps the ancient nature of the pagan mother goddess here accounts for this breaking away from the Vedic rule. In any case, the *garba grha* is fascinating for its wall panels are of images associated with Tantric rites, not commonly seen any more in India.

Rajarani

This graceful but unfinished yellow sandstone temple, which was in all probability never used since its deity was not installed, has a curious name. Rajarani means king and queen, so the shrine is often mistakenly considered to have been named after its royal patron and his wife. The truth of the matter is that it actually refers to the stone employed in its construction, called *rajrania* in the vernacular.

A later temple of the Orissan period, perhaps to be dedicated to Vishnu and built in the 12th century AD, Rajarani reflects the sophistication which the local architects had managed to achieve over the 400 years of temple building in the state. Indeed, scholars are of the opinion that Rajarani falls more in the category of the Khajuraho group than the Orissa one.

The whole temple is ornately carved with artistic sculpture featuring an unusual delicacy of human figures. Traditional carved *ashtadikpala*-s guard the cardinal points around the temple, two at each side. They are surrounded by images of minor gods, goddesses, celebrants and animals, a feast for the eyes. The superbly carved bodies are slimmer and more proportionate than usual and seem to move unaffectedly rather than in the deliberate, stylized and symbolic fashion often associated with Indian gods.

The unusual thing about Rajarani is its 55 foot high convoluted tower. This is not in fact, a single structure but rather a multitude of smaller *vimana*-s, crowding together like supplicants praying for a sight of god. They combine to create one huge vertical but round block, though the plan is square at the base. The effect is far from monolithic or oppressive for it is relieved by dainty carvings over each tiny spire.

The complex and elaborate filigree work that Oriya artisans create even today in their silver jewellery, seems almost to be rooted in the delicate lacy designs of the Rajarani and its contemporaries. Each superstructure is fully worked, rising from a slightly plainer platform to a heavily decorated column which reveals a panoply of gods and fertility goddesses with a background of tracery, blending with various elements of nature and birth — trees, leaves, flowers, geese, peacocks, elephants, lilies and other blossoms, and even children.

On the walls of the unfinished *antarala* with its figures of *naga*-s and *nagini*-s (male and female snake gods), are blocked out or drawn designs for the *shilpin* (artisan) to carve out. What happened to those craftsmen? Why was the Rajarani left incomplete and unsanctified? It is just one more puzzle in the mysterious history of Hindu architecture.

JAGANNATHA AT PURI

A restless king, an impatient queen and a mysterious statue are behind the great temple of Krishna, the Jagannatha or 'Lord of the Universe', at Purushottamkshetra or Puri. It was once part of a kingdom ruled by the great King Indradyumna, who, having obtained every earthly success, desired to create something that would make him immortal.

"I shall build a temple," the king thought, "but whom do I build it for?" A dream supplied the answer. Indradyumna dreamt of an exquisite statue of Jagannatha, which sat hidden from the world in its cave shrine on a hill called Nilachala. But he had no way of knowing where to find Nilachala or indeed the Nilamadhava (the blue Madhava or Krishna) image. So his trusted forces were sent out into the countryside on this mission. One young soldier named Vidyapati discovered, by trickery, the whereabouts of the cave and stole the idol, which belonged to a hermit named Viswavasu, for his king.

However, the devotee of Nilamadhava fell into utter despair when he discovered his god missing. Krishna, seeing his plight, returned to the cave as the image, much to Indradyumna's chagrin. Still, the ruler's piety too was rewarded when Krishna called out to him from the heavens reassuring him that he

Puri ~ Home of the Lord of the Universe

Puri – Home of the Lord of the Universe

would be given his own idol. "But do you have a temple to house the Lord in?" asked Krishna. "First build a shrine, then will your god come to you."

The royal architects spent many years in the construction of the Jagannatha temple. When it was complete, Krishna reappeared before the king and told him to pick up from the sea a log that he would find floating upon it. Neither Indradyumna nor anyone else could lift the strange log, so the devoted Viswavasu was summoned. Such was the strength of his devotion that he picked it up as if it were a feather.

Now Indradyumna had to have an image carved on this sacred piece of wood. All the artisans of the kingdom were unwilling to take on such a mighty task. Finally, an old man came to the king agreeing to carve a statue of Jagannatha, his brother Balaram and sister, Subhadra, on the condition that he had complete privacy and three weeks' time to do his work in. No one would be allowed to see the images in the meantime.

His locked workroom, of course, proved to be too much of a temptation for Indradyumna's inquisitive wife. One day, not being able to hear the sound of wood being chipped away, she thought she had better look in and make sure that all was well. As soon as she did so, the old man - perhaps Krishna himself — vanished into thin air and the images were left unfinished. The king, however, was happy with the deities as they were and proceeded to install them at the new shrine. And from that time onward, Vishnu, in the incarnation of Krishna, came to be worshipped at the seaside town of Puri.

Historians date the present shrine at 1198 A.D. The conical tower of the grand monument stands over 170 feet high and is topped by the traditional flag hoisted when a Hindu shrine is completed. The *shikhara* also bears the wheel of Vishnu, visible to boats far out at sea. An 18 foot wall encloses a massive square space which measures nearly 600 feet on each side. Within this, a small enclosure contains the whitewashed sanctum.

This medieval temple is much larger than the one that inspired it, the Lingaraja of Bhubaneshwar, barely 24 miles away. Sometimes thought to have been originally built as a

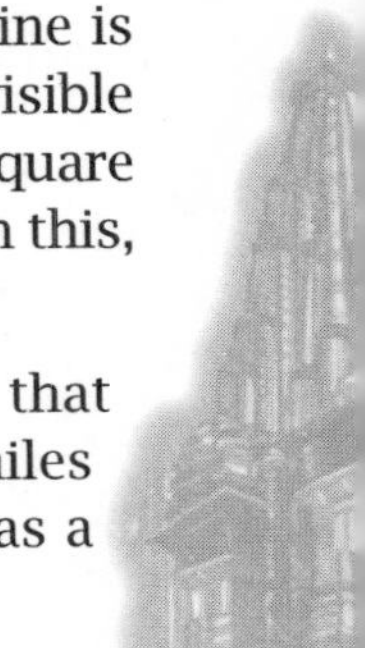

tower of victory by Cheda Ganga Dev in the year 1030 AD, Jagannatha was only sanctified as a place of worship years later. As an architectural work, it is not extraordinary nor innovative though it does contain the lace work style of carving peculiar to Orissa. More dear to the pilgrim than the tourist, Jagannatha is open to all Hindus, regardless of caste.

Non-Hindus are, unfortunately, not allowed to enter the Jagannatha estate. Once a fair-skinned Indian accompanying a Western friend was barred from going in because priests insisted he was a 'foreigner'. This did not prevent the priests from requesting him for a donation. The non-Hindu tourist can get a glimpse of the main shrine from a platform similar to the one at Bhubaneshwar. Also visible from here is the beautiful Garuda pillar in front of the *deul*, and the smaller shrines on the estate, which vary in design and dimension and were constructed over the ages by wealthy worshippers.

On a single axis running from east to west, the Jagannatha consists of four chambers. The *bhog* and *nat mandir*-s were constructed in the 14th or 15th centuries, much after the *jagmohan* and *deul* were built. Both the offering and dance hall are replete with decoration. Their walls are filled with stylized images of the oft-seen auxiliary deities and attendants.

The *jagmohan* of Jagannatha has 16 pillars, a rarity. The entrance to the shrine is enriched with sculpted scenes from Krishna's life, telling the tale of the god's many mischievous escapades and its gates and walls are embellished with marble figures of lions and guards. The images in the *deul* are unusual with odd, monkey-like, innocent faces. The statue of Subhadra lacks arms because of her creator's hasty departure from Puri.

The temple complex, guarded by a lion gateway, is approached by a wide road constructed up to the Gundicha Mandir, a little over a mile away, en route to the Sun Temple at Konark. Every June, hordes of pilgrims swarm the city as the idols of the Jagannatha are ritually prepared, attended by some 6,000 men, for a journey to the Gundicha Mandir. Here they rest for seven days before being brought back to their original location. The symbolic trip, undertaken by the gods in three wooden, 16 wheeled cars, celebrates the occasion of Krishna's legendary journey from Gokul to Mathura.

Interestingly, a little-known town called Mahesh in West Bengal, also has a large, ancient Jagannatha shrine. Every year, at the same time as the Puri car festival, a grand *rath yatra* of the deity takes place at Mahesh.

KONARK

The colossal ruins amidst the sands at Konark are all that remain of an ambitious temple complex in glimmering black stone, built in the 13th century AD. Seeing them brings flashes of Percy Bysshe Shelley's poem, *Ozymandias*, to mind:

I met a traveller from an antique land
Who said: Two vast and trunkless legs of stone
Stand in the desert...
Nothing beside remains. Round the decay
Of that colossal wreck, boundless and bare,
the lone and level sands stretch far away.

This Surya temple, which mariners once relied on as a landmark, is constructed at what must have been the great Oriya port city alluded to by Ptolemy in his geography of India. It epitomizes the peak of the skill and talent that the architects and craftsmen of Orissa had achieved in the 'middle ages'. Its refined style signifies the zenith of centuries of building at Bhubaneshwar and Puri. Konark is world-famous for two reasons; the first, its exquisite sculpture and grandeur; the second, its collection of erotic carvings in the manner of the Khajuraho group.

Its patron was probably the Ganga king, Narsimha Deva I, who might have built the shrine as a celebration of the defence of his kingdom against Muslim invaders. It supposedly took 12 years to build and may, in fact, never have been completed. Certainly it was planned on a splendid scale by its architect, Bishu Maharana. This is clear even from its ruins.

The estate stands 1.8 miles from the coast in a walled compound measuring 875 by 540 feet, with entry possible through three gateways, the main one boasting two stone lions crushing elephants. Konark consists of the chief chariot temple, a separate *nat* or *bhog mandir*, statuary including near life-size elephants to the north and horses to the south, as well as subsidiary shrines like the one to a deity named Mayadevi. The grounds must also have housed the more practical structures associated with a religious site — the refectory, kitchens, and store houses — but none of these are standing today.

Bishu Maharana visualized the abode of the Sun God in the form of the deity's vehicle. So the *deul* and three subsidiary shrines are attached to the *jagmohan* (with its 100 foot high roof), the whole thing structured as a chariot. Its interior contains the *garba grha*, now without a holy idol. The variety of sculpture on the exterior is intended to exalt the viewer and bring his attention to the power and strength of god.

The base of the carved car has 24 wheels, each 10 feet high, with eight spokes. Within each of the spokes is carved a couple in an erotic pose or *sthambha*. Behind them, all along the plinth and rising up the walls and roof are the remaining erotic carvings. Other recurring motifs on the walls include various animals like lion and elephants in continuous friezes rather like primitive negatives of film. Also there are bevies of female attendants for the sun god who seemed to prefer worshippers of the fairer sex.

In front of the chariot are the seven great horses who strain to pull the weight of the structure. One might see them froth at the mouth. The other exquisite yet contrasting sculpture at the site consists of three green chlorite statues of Surya, aligned in such a manner that they catch the sun at dawn, noon, and sunset. This is why locals insist that the temple be seen at all three times of the day and indeed there are special sunrise and sunset tours to Konark.

The chlorite figures are so finely worked that they make the exquisitely carved horses appear coarse in comparison. The quality of these carvings is unrivalled; with their peculiar colouring and beautiful workmanship, they resemble bronzes. The splendid detail on the body of Surya is breathtaking. From the carving, the god appears to be wearing gossamer thin cloth on which even the embroidery is discernible. His rich waist belt glows gold in the sun and one feels his skin would be warm to the touch.

The *shikhara* of the temple was meant to be at least 225 feet tall. Legend has it that when the temple was almost ready, the architects found they could not figure out how to place the *amalaka* atop the spire. The chief architect's young son, Dharmapada, had just arrived at Konark to meet, for the first time, his father who had been away on site for years.

The 16 year old boy had also studied the holy architecture texts and with the *sastra*-s fresh in his mind, he was able to discover a way to set the *amalaka*. The architects listened to him and accordingly raised the crown. Apparently though, their pride could not tolerate the fact that a novice had succeeded where they had failed. So Dharmapada climbed to the top of the mighty temple and threw himself into the ocean sacrificing himself so his elders would save face.

The truth seems to be that no matter how stunning the temple was in artistic terms, as an engineering feat, it was at least a partial failure. Although the three-tiered roof of the temple was reinforced with wrought iron girders to enable them to take the weight of the stone *shikhara*, it is unlikely that the workers were ever able to build the tower to the intended height. The stones were just too heavy. Indeed, what is marvellous is the accomplishment of transporting at all such massive blocks here in that day and age from 80 miles away.

Also, the stones were not held in place so much by mortar or iron grips but simply by balancing them in a particular way. If the finial had not been so heavy, perhaps this would have worked. Anyhow, in the sandy soil the foundations may have shifted during construction, thereby sinking the structure and causing its weakness. Part of the *shikhara* is said to have been "standing in 1837, but by 1869 had collapsed." [2] Nonetheless, this temple devoted to the Sun is one of a kind. If its ruins can arouse such awe, perhaps Bishu Maharana achieved what he set out to do.

BENGAL

Bengal has played a considerable role in India's history. From ancient times, when it was home to the bustling port city of Tamaralipti, which traded with the east Asian countries, right up to the independence struggle in the early part of the 20th century, when it gave the nation intellectuals and freedom fighters like Raja Ram Mohan Roy, Rabindranath Tagore, Swami Vivekananda and Subhash Chandra Bose.

Unfortunately, as much as the state filled India's coffers in terms of literature, art and music, its overall contribution to architecture has been arguably slight. The topography and climate of Bengal, like Kerala and Kashmir, and its distancing, due to geographical factors, from the evolution of the Nagara tradition, ensured the development of a unique indigenous style of religious architecture. However, frustratingly, just as in Kashmir few temples survive, so also in Bengal many ancient shrines have disappeared. In a region prone to flooding, where perishable construction materials like brick, clay and bamboo were largely used, it was only natural that buildings would be unable to withstand the vagaries of nature.

KALIGHAT

The most renowned temple of Bengal then, is perhaps the one that has given its name to the state capital, Calcutta. The 300 year old city owes its existence, at least partially, to a toe. The toe of Sati, whose body made this land sacred.

One summer evening, a Brahmin was praying on the banks of the Bhagirathi (another name for the Ganga, named after the sage who prayed to Siva to send water to the needy earth). When he had finished his worship, he bent down to the water to wash his face. In the twilight, he could glimpse something shining brightly under the river's surface. It was too dark to venture into the river so, containing his impatience, the man went home.

The next morning, with the sun lending his assistance, the Brahmin searched at the spot for the mysterious source of light. Imagine his surprise when, through the clear water, he discerned a gleaming toe of stone. Although the man had no idea where the toe had come from, he began to worship it in the forest until one day, while asleep, he dreamt of the story of Siva's devoted wife Sati, how she had died, and how Vishnu had scattered her body across the land.

So the priest built a modest temple to worship the relic. At some later date the shrine was probably rebuilt in a grander way. As it often transpires, the news of a temple brought people flocking to the region and a village grew on the banks of the Bhagirathi. The temple began to be called Kalighat after the goddess Kali. And when the British colonizers moved their trading post 23 miles down the Hoogly river to the villages of Sutanati, Govindpur and Kalighat, then was Calcutta born.

The Kalighat temple, however, apart from its historical and mythological significance is neither an architectural masterpiece nor a famous *tirtha*. It was rebuilt in the 19th century and in order to appease the bloodthirsty nature of the warrior goddess, goats are sacrificed here. To its north is the better-known Dakshineshwar temple, singular in that it is supposedly the only site in the country where a Siva and Kali shrine are located in the same estate. Principally a Kali temple, Dakshineshwar, meaning Lord of the South, possesses 12 small Siva shrines in its compound and was constructed in 1847. It was renowned for being frequented by the 20th century philosopher and religious leader, Ramakrishna Parmahamsa.

It may be that the less widely-known temples of Bengal, at Bishnupur, Bansberia and Maynapur, present more characteristic examples of the regional style. They are unique in their construction and design, especially their use of terra-cotta tiles.

The temple of Bengal was a rectangular room fronted by a sloping roofed verandah, ideal against the rain, which derived from the traditional vernacular mud and bamboo hut called the *bangaldar* (the word *bangla* meaning house, hence bungalow, obtains from this region). From this, in turn, was developed the building with the *do-chala* or pitched roof, which had a rectangular sanctum and the *chou-chala* or hipped roof style, with a square one. Although the essential structure was of brick, architects used stone or wood for such sections as doorways, windows or pillars but covered them with the red blocks to prevent weathering by the elements.

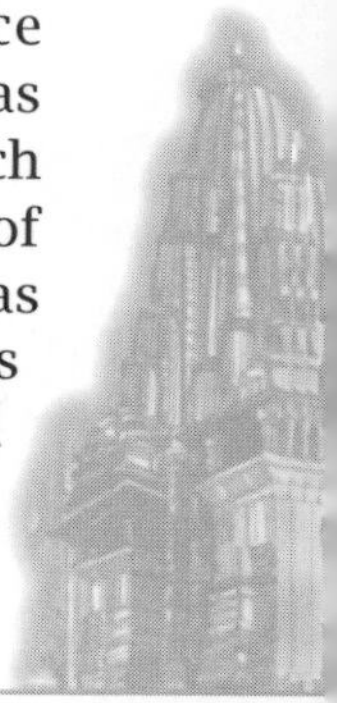

BISHNUPUR

A town about 60 miles north-west of Calcutta, in the Bankura district, Bishnupur was the seat of Malla rulers from the 16th to the early 19th century. Since no stone was available in the vicinity, builders utilized bricks made from the local mud in the construction of all important buildings. Examples of this brick work exists in the 17th century temples of the area, especially worth seeing in the Keshta Raya, Jor Bangla, Ras Mancha and Madan Mohan shrines.

The *do-chala* Keshta Raya temple, built in 1643 AD and dedicated to Krishna, seems Islamic in design. This is probably due to the fact that it was constructed at a time when Muslim rulers had already had a great effect on the art, architecture, literature and lifestyle of the whole northern part of the Indian sub-continent.

Built on a characteristic platform or plinth, its ornate walls rise up, windowless, to meet two tiled roofs between which is placed a small tower, with a similar covering. The exterior of the shrine is also studded with terra-cotta tiles but these are especially decorated with intricate local motifs, scenes from Hindu mythology and vernacular icons of the gods, to add a touch of lightness to the heavy red structure.

BANSBERIA

This small town might be, for all you know, in Russia, if its name and its religious architecture are anything to go by. But the sleepy little hamlet is very much a part of Bengal, only 28 miles north of Calcutta. It is known only for its two temples, the Ananta-Vasudeva and the Hamseshvari, belonging to the 17th or 18th century.

The smaller temple of Ananta-Vasudeva fits in with the style of Bishnupur although it possesses but one roof from the middle of which rises a squat tower. Its three arched patio and brick detail is reminiscent of a Mughal tomb. The other temple of Bansberia calls to mind the Kremlin or similar such Russian or Turkish buildings with their minarets rising up in a fashion most uncommon to Hindu architecture. Here

The Great Temple Somnath

In Soreth are jewels five
horses, rivers, women;
Somnath the fourth;
Fifth Huree's presence.

...It is a holy land, to the Jain the land of Adeenath and Urisht Nemee,
to the orthodox Hindoo the country of Mahadeva and Shree Krishn...

The Great Temple Somnath

In Soreth are jewels five
horses, rivers, women;
Somnath the fourth;
Fifth Huree's presence.

...It is a holy land, to the Jain the land of Adeenath and Urisht Neme,
to the orthodox Hindoo the country of Mahadeva and Shree Krishn...

The Land of the Moon

The Temples of the West

Gujarat — Somnath, Dwaraka, Gop, Ghumli, Modhera;
Rajasthan — Pushkar, Osian

Gujarat

This is the land of Lothal, city of the ancient Harappans. The land where Krishna, the mischievous cowherd god, spent much of his illustrious life and where he died. The land where many sacred sites of the Jaina sect are located. That land which, jutting out into the Arabian Sea, forms the westernmost frontier of post-independence India. Gujarat.

The modern state of Gujarat now consists of an eastern mainland, the peninsular region of Kathiawar, and the more isolated Rann of Kachchh on the border of Pakistan. Kathiawar, known in ancient times as Saurashtra, had an extraordinary link with the people of Kashmir, a factor which greatly influenced its ancient temple tradition. Here, along the coast and some of the areas inland, many of the great events in Krishna's life occurred and some of India's greatest temples were built.

Unfortunately, Muslim invaders responsible for the destruction of many religious buildings in northern India made especially severe, repeated and concentrated attacks on the wealthy temple sites of Gujarat. The result? More ruins and documentation than the legendary temples themselves. The apparently spectacular shrines had been constructed by the early Maitrika clan and the productive builders of the Solanki dynasty. They were responsible for many of the great Hindu and Jaina shrines of the region, erected in the eras both prior to, and after, the Sultanate period.

The temples of both religions in Gujarat were ornate and well planned. The wealthy mercantile community possessed the taste and could afford the resources required for such elaborate structures as the ones on Mount Abu and Satrunjaya Hill. Mainly Nagara in style, the temples responded to the region's warm, dry climate by being airy and well lit, often with unenclosed *mandapa-s* adorned with fabulously carved pillars and high, coffered ceilings. Their openness and the use of locally available materials like marble, and yellow, red, or brown sandstone, added to the temples' delicacy and enabled sculpture to be complex but also buoyant and graceful.

The early architecture of Saurashtra was greatly influenced by its northern immigrants while later Gujarati architecture reflected the predominant Jaina trend of the area. Between the two there was little similarity or connection, separated as they were by time. The former was vernacular in style and devoted to deities like the sun, while the latter, though dedicated to the *tirthankara* or Jaina saints, incorporated mainstream Hindu Nagara elements in its medieval structures.

SOMNATH

The legendary and rare temple of the Lord of the Moon, is also the temple of nine lives. Destroyed repeatedly, its generations of devotees have persevered and rebuilt it time and again. Whether in a state of ruin or not, its sanctity was never forgotten.

Somnath-Patan is believed to be so very ancient that it witnessed the creation of the universe. One legend states that it was first built by Soma, the moon god, in gold; then by Ravana in silver; and a third time by Krishna, in wood. The more plausible explanation is that it was first constructed in the 6th century AD during the reign of Bhimadeva.

The story and reason for the temple's location is intriguing. The moon was, along with Siva, among the 50 sons-in-law of King Daksha. The king seemed to have held a grudge against many of his daughters' husbands. One day, angered by the radiant Soma's disobedience, Daksha cursed him, saying that his brilliance would be dimmed forever. And sure enough, from that day Soma started to disappear. The gods, frightened that the world would be in total darkness every night, beseeched Daksha to take back his words.

Time had cooled the king's fury so he told his son-in-law that he would be saved if he bathed at the confluence of the river Saraswati and the sea at Patan and then prayed to Siva. This he did and regained his light. Still, every month his light diminishes and on *amavasya* (no moon) night, Soma must return to the temple of his Lord, Siva (Somnath) and bathe in the holy waters of the river to become radiant once more.

So the original site of the temple was located where Soma worshipped the Siva *linga*. In the eastern part of the town of Patan, it stood by the seashore separated from the water by a retaining wall. The temple was famed for its *jyotir* (light/the lit one) *linga*-s, one of 12 special, sacred Siva *linga-s* in the country. The others are variously located at Srisailam, Ujjain, Devgadh, Rameshwaram, Bhimashankara, Triambak near Nasik, Grishneshwar near Ellora, Kedarnath, Kashi, Mandhata, and Darukavana.

Somnath was first sacked by Mahmud of Ghazni in 1025 AD and according to noted Indian historian, Romila Thapar, its "effects were to remain for centuries in the Hindu mind and to colour its assessment of the character of Mahmud, and on occasion, of Muslim rulers in general".[1] The plunderer had come in search of gold and idols to destroy. Ironically he did not quite succeed. Some remnants of the

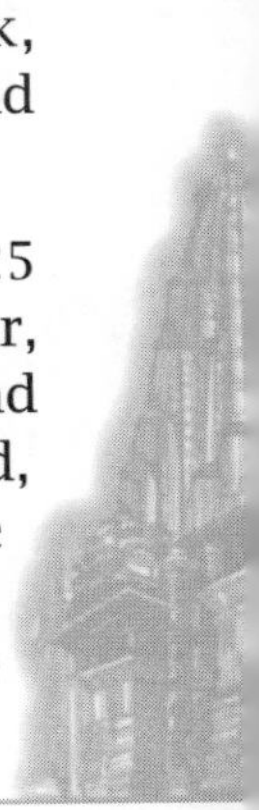

original structure of Somnath were utilized in the Maipuri mosque (at the site of another temple that Mahmud had torn down), despite the fact that they still bore religious sculptures and motifs. This use of Hindu temple walls, ceilings and panels in the Islamic places of worship in the Sultanate continued inexplicably and against the very motives of the invaders, throughout the medieval period in Gujarat. Inadvertently, the oversight blended two religions while keeping the art of the temple tradition alive.

The Somnath Siva *linga* always escaped destruction, being whisked away from the temple whenever it was in danger, for it was attacked again in 1297, 1394 and 1706 AD. For a time, the priests kept the *linga* hidden, only installing it for worship when Rani Ahilya Bai Holkar ordered a new shrine made, with a secret *garba grha*, in the late 18th century. Still, the new temple is hardly a memorial to the grand original and is usually only visited by devout pilgrims.

The original was famed as indescribably exquisite and rich. Although only one storey high, Somnath was large in scale. It had a closed, central hall — *gridhamandapa* — with three entrances fronted by shady porticos. The hall's intricately worked ceiling now graces the Maipuri mosque. The sanctum sanctorum, in which the idol is said to have floated but was probably controlled by some magnetic mechanism, was to the west of the hall. It had a wide circumambulatory, lit by big window-balconies, like the oriel or balcony windows of Khajuraho.

At Patan there was also the ancient Triveni sun temple, distinguished by the three sets of niches around its ambulatory, meant for the figures of the three divine couples — Vishnu and Lakshmi; Brahma and Saraswati; Siva and Parvati.

DWARAKA

Dwaraka was the legendary kingdom of Krishna, and therefore one of the four holiest *tirtha sthana-s* or *dham-s* (centres of pilgrimage) in India. The site for the beautiful town was chosen by the dark-skinned god, designed by the divine architect, Vishwakarma, and constructed by labourers sent to the earth from both heaven and hell. Krishna ruled there till his death, when a curse on him brought about the city's destruction as well.

Years after the great war that was waged by the Pandava princes and Krishna against their cousins, the Kauravas (as recounted in the *Mahabharata*), a hunter mistook a slumbering Krishna for a deer and killed him with his arrow. Then came the deluge and Dwaraka disappeared beneath the waves. But the land was so holy that it could not remain lost forever. Archaeologists have found that new towns have been built upon the same site at least five times.

The small town which comes alive every year during *Janmashtami*, Krishna's birthday, is the location of his Dwarakanath temple. It was supposedly built by one of his descendants, Vajranath, and is the place where Krishna's renowned devotee, Mira Bai, a Rajput princess, gave herself up to the god, disappearing one night in the sanctum sanctorum. The only trace left of her was her saree hanging upon the image of her beloved Hari.

Gop

Gop is a unique site for it represents the oldest surviving shrine in Kathiawar and is an uncanny likeness of the Martanda Surya temple of Kashmir. Built by the ancient Maitrika dynasty, which reigned from 470 to 748 AD, it belongs to the minority of regional shrines (alongside those of Kashmir and Bengal) in a fleeting but distinctive tradition.

The peninsula of Saurashtra, separated from the mainland of central India but accessible from the north, provided a cul-de-sac to northern tribes retreating from Kashmir, Sindh, and Rajputana or exploring new territories south of their own. These people brought to Gujarat not only their lifestyles and religious preferences but also their deities, modes of worship, and building patterns. On the coast where they settled, they created artistic marvels in stone. Their effect was clearly seen in the popular ancient tradition of sun worship. The temple of Gop is an outstanding example. Sober in style, it possessed the pyramidal, pitched roof of the Kashmiri tradition, though in the Gujarat

weather there was no necessity for such a covering. Rising above the sanctum and *pradakshina* path, its roof was layered and relieved by purely decorative windows and 'low clerestories'.

GHUMLI

Built in the Barda Hills, where the Rajput Jethwa princes ruled from the 10th to the 14th centuries is the fine medieval Navlakha temple of Ghumli. A large, open, two-storeyed structure, unlike the closed plan of the hall of old Somnath, Ghumli is but two thirds the width and length of the temple of the Lord of the Moon.

Square in plan, with octagonal sides forming recesses, this early but grand 13th century shrine is built on a high plinth. Adorned by oriel windows, it was one of the last shrines built enthusiastically by the Solankis before their domination by the Sultanate rulers.

MODHERA

King Bhimadeva I, who ruled the Saurashtra region in the 11th century AD, is said to have built the beautifully carved sun temple at Modhera, north of Kathiawar, between 1026 and 1027. Built in front of a rectangular tank (which has small shrines at three of its sides), Modhera is a precursor of the Sun temple at Konark. The similarity between the two is evident in that the idols were installed to be naturally lit by the sun. In the case of Modhera, the icon was placed so that it was bathed in light at the time of the equinoxes.

The large, stepped, stone *kund* with recesses for small images of subsidiary deities, leads up a staircase to a *torana*, with fine, broad-based pillars sans their joining arch. The now spireless shrine, built on a raised platform, is entered through a great, octagonal, pillared pavilion carved in the lavish fashion favoured by the Solankis. At a distance the pillars give the appearance of solid mass. Close up, they produce exactly the opposite effect, so finely carved and full of detail are they. As in other Surya temples, the carvings are predominantly of female attendants. Rows of frames carved out on each pillar hold graceful dancing figures as well as the plump *gana-s* or *yaksha-s* that seem to hover around the gods.

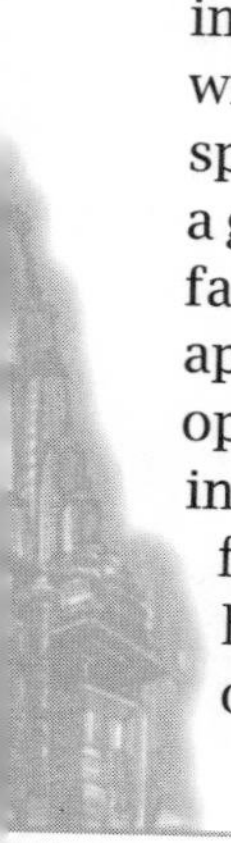

Modhera ~ House of the Sun

Modhera – House of the Sun

A separate structure from this pavilion is the closed *mandapa* beyond it leading to the *pradakshina* path and *garba grha.* The temple may once have had more than one level but in its state of ruin it is difficult to tell. Recurring images of the sun god appear at important positions throughout the structure, especially on the 'dedicatory block above the *mandapa* doorway'. In Modhera too, as in Kashmir, the representation of the sun god seems to indicate a foreign model for the figure is clothed for cold weather in boots and cloak, unfamiliar to Gujarat. However, the main idol, and his sunken *garba grha,* are lost to us forever. It is fortunate that his chariot pulled by seven horses was drawn from the rubble around the temple before it could be further ruined.

Although the temple's *shikhara* is missing, the spires of the small *kund* temples are an indication of what it might have looked like. Even though probably more curvilinear than those of Konark or Khajuraho, Modhera's spire followed the basic Nagara pattern of vertical lines meeting at a point directly above the *garba grha.*

RAJASTHAN

The temple architecture of Rajputana is closely linked with that of Gujarat, formal state boundaries being a fairly recent phenomenon. The Pratihara dynasty of the 8th to 10th centuries, established their capital at Kanauj and ruled from there until their defeat by the same invaders who had wreaked havoc on the temple architecture of Gujarat.

Much of the Pratihara heritage was destroyed. However, enough examples exist at sites like Osian, Roda and Chittor to indicate the architectural developments they were responsible for. The early temples of the Pratiharas evolved from simple structures consisting of a *garba grha* (also called *mula prasada* in this region) and a porch, aligned on an east-west axis, opening towards the east into more complex shrines with vestibules, a series of open or closed *mandapa-s* for dancing, square in plan and supported by nine pillars, or oblong, divided by aisles.

Early square pillars develop into elaborate, composite ones — square, octagonal or sixteen-sided at the base, while plain ceilings become ornate, adorned often with a central lotus motif. The temples were well lit and ventilated by deep porches and balconies, an element later to be seen in the palaces of Rajasthan as well.

Pushkar

The only major Brahma temple in the country is located in Rajasthan. Legend has it that the god himself chose the location. Perhaps he thought his curse would not hold good in the sleepy desert town of Pushkar. His multi-coloured temple, guarded by his faithful animal vehicle, the swan (*hans*), and the local camel fair or Pushkar Mela, are the only claims to fame this sleepy hollow of a town makes.

Osian

The 16 temples at Osian, an oasis in the Thar desert, 33 miles from Jodhpur, represent both the early and developed works of the Pratihara. These include the Hari Hara group of temples ranging from the almost primitive Pipla Mata to the more ornate Sun temples. Built on large raised foundations, a pattern that was becoming more and more common in the Nagara style, many of these structures are *panchayatana*, increasing in intricacy and sculpted work with time (see Gwalior and Gyraspur, Chapter 4).

Note

1 *The History of India*, Romila Thapar, Volume I, Penguin India, Calcutta, 1990

The Lad Khan ~ Aihole

I bow to thee! Oh Anant or Vishnu, who hast a thousand images, a thousand feet, eyes, heads, chests and shoulders, who hast a thousand names and who art eternal and who hast outlived crores of eras, I bow to thee.

Traditional Marathi pilgrim's invocation to God

The Lad Khan - Aihole

I bow to thee! Oh Anant or Vishnu, who hast a thousand
images, a thousand feet, eyes, heads, chests and shoulders,
who hast a thousand names and who art eternal
and who hast outlived crores of eras, I bow to thee.

Traditional Marathi pilgrim's invocation to God

The Melting Pot

Temples of the Deccan

Mumbai — Elephanta; **Ellora** — Kailashnath; **Pandharpur** — Vithoba, Taak Pithya; **Aihole** — Lad Khan, Durga; **Pattadakal** — Virupaksha; **Hampi** — Hazara Rama; **Somnathapur** — Chenna Keshava

The vast expanse of land known as the *Deccan* (meaning southern), actually contains the geographical centre of India. It stretches over four states; Maharashtra, Goa, the western part of Andhra Pradesh and Karnataka, and separates north India from the south. Classifying temples is a complex and, especially in the case of the Deccan, rather unjust thing to do. The Deccan includes a rich spectrum of religious buildings from as far north as Ellora (Maharashtra) to as far south as Somnathapur (southern Karnataka) and dating from the 2nd century BC to as late as the 17th century AD.

This territory, ruled variously by the early Vakataka, the Kalachuri of Maharashtra and the Chalukya of Karnataka, the Yadava, the Rashtrakuta, and then the Kadamba dynasties, continuously acted as a filter between the northern and southern cultures, ultimately absorbing much of both. It not only includes structures in both the Nagara and Dravida styles but also its own hybrid, the Chalukyan style. The great Deccan region was famous for this rich tradition, initiated around the same time as that of the Pallavas in southern India; for the grandeur of its ancient Buddhist and Jaina shrines; and the splendour of its Vijayanagara cities.

The hardy Chalukyans were the rulers who took Hindu architecture beyond the realms of the mighty Gupta empire in the 5th century. They consolidated their dominion despite threats of foreign invasion from the north and hints of trouble with their neighbours, the Rashtrakutas. During their long reign, two phases of building activity occurred, the first being from 450-700 AD, the second lasting from the 11th to the 14th centuries AD.

The signficant difference between the architecturally important temples of the Deccan — sometimes called Deccani, attesting to their amalgam of northern and southern elements — and those of southern India, is that while a large number of the latter are centres of great temple towns, still used and venerated, many of the former belong to long-gone empires and dead cities. Therefore, perhaps, they appear more ancient and distanced from the visitor.

Such is the case of the Hoysala temples of Halebid and Belur, the Chalukyan shrines of Badami or some of the austere Yadava Hemadpanti temples of southern Maharashtra near the Karnataka border. Though the superb 11th century Ambarnath temple, also in Maharashtra, is still in use, it suffers from lack of maintenance.

It must be remembered that in the Deccan, as anywhere else in India, there are also numerous smaller temples that may be architecturally or historically less notable than many of those featured in this book. Nonetheless, in terms of religion, they are dear to the local people and thus of great importance. These include temples like the one where the poet-saint, Jnaneshwar is celebrated, at Alandi in Maharashtra and Goan temples such as the oft-visited Mangeshi and Shantadurga. Many are devoted to local deities that are an amalgam of traditional Hindu gods with older regional ones.

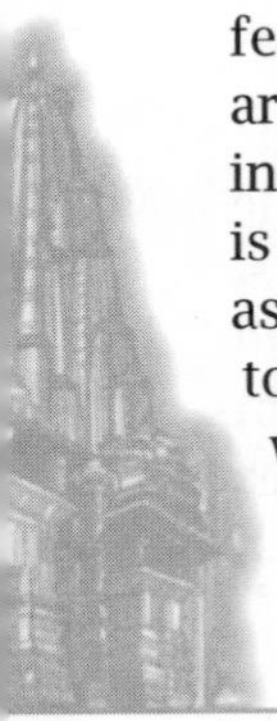

Another temple worthy of mention as a religious site is the relatively young shrine of Sai Baba in Shirdi, close to Nasik in Maharashtra. The people of modern India flock to this new *tirtha* to ask the blessing of the 'latter-day' saint who embodies the essence of national integration. The small town sprang up, purely for economic reasons, around the temple. Nearby Nasik is also often visited for its shrines. It is also one of the four venues of the Kumbh Mela (see Hardwar, Chapter 4,).

Elephanta at Mumbai

The magnificent cave temples, with their mammoth and awe-inspiring sculptures, on the island of Gharapuri (the island of elephants), are a world heritage site. Despite this status and their popularity among tourists, the Saivite shrines, cut between 450-750 AD, continue to be desecrated by vandals unconcerned about their historical and religious significance.

The defacementof monuments is not a recent phenomenon. The religiously intolerant Portuguese (who first arrived in India in 1498, when Vasco da Gama landed in Kerala), disfigured many Indian shrines and sculptures. Among the unfortunate sites was Gharapuri. Ironically, it was these same Portuguese who gave the island the name it bears even today — Elephanta.

It is reached by way of ferry from Bombay's Apollo Bunder harbour. From the landing dock, a flight of stairs leads the visitor to the caves. Apart from the chief temple, there is a smaller *linga* shrine. The large shrine is cruciform in plan, with beautiful and moving panels carved in the *mandapa* fronting the *garba grha.*

These powerful 'murals' which echo Siva's moods and strength, also detail his life and forms; from his marriage to Parvati to his potent *Tandava Nritya* that shook the world, from his hermaphrodite *avatar* of *Ardhanarishwara,* the half-woman-half-man god who represents the two aspects of human beings — *anima* and *animus,* masculine and feminine, passive force and active, contrasting yet analogous halves of each person, to the splendid sculpture of the Trimurti on the south wall of the cave.

ELLORA

By the beginning of the 7th century AD, free-standing structures had come into their own but Jaina, Buddhist and Hindu rock-cut shrines continued to be popular for three centuries or so more. Not far from Ajanta[1], there began to be cut, in a two mile stretch of north-south hillside at Ellora, the columned halls favoured by contemporary Hindus and Buddhists.

The Rashtrakutas, who had defeated one branch of the Chalukyas, were the patrons of these cave shrines, carving the important ones like the Dashavatara, the Rameshwara and the Ravana-ki-khai,each a must-see. Of the 34 cave shrines at Ellora, 17 are Hindu.

KAILASHNATH

The one monumental structure on the Ellora hill range is the monolithic Kailashnath shrine of Siva, representing the mountain abode of the destroyer and therefore appropriately born of the rocky cliff itself and unsupported by any extraneous fortifying elements.

It is a common misconception that Kailashnath, dedicated to Siva and hewn between 760 and 800 AD, is a cave. In reality, the whole structure was carved out of the hill to be a free-standing temple, detached from all three sides of its mother rock and, according to a noted documentarian of Indian architecture, covers twice the area of the Parthenon in Athens and is one and a half times as high. If there were to be an eighth wonder of the world, this could be it.

To create this marvel of engineering and artistry, with its complex plan, including various galleries and levels and its unforgettable and extensive carvings, a pit was dug into the ground to produce a courtyard 300 feet long and 175 feet wide, within which was cut a block of basalt, measuring 250 by 150 feet and standing 100 feet high. This was ingeniously carved from the top downwards omitting the necessity of scaffolding. Unlike its cave neighbours, the Kailashnath being open to the sky and standing on a plinth 25 feet high, is lit

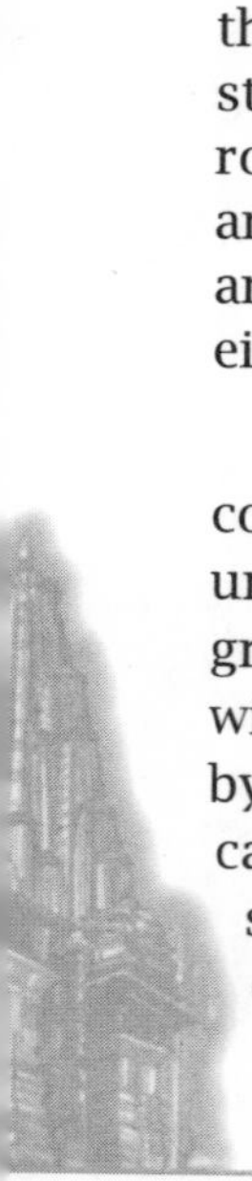

even within its deep interiors. Lighting is also aided by the strategic placement of terraces, balconies, and courtyards.

Although modern-day visitors may admire the dark rock of the three-tiered, 95 foot high Rashtrakuta shrine, it is likely that after construction it was embellished with paint as indeed were many temples which now appear to be bare stone. The labyrinthine complex can be divided into four basic segments — the principal Siva shrine; its west-facing entranceway; a shrine for Siva's faithful vehicle, Nandi; and a courtyard set with cloisters.

The main place of worship is the customary square sanctum with a massive Siva *linga*, an *antarala*, and a sixteen-pillared *mahamandapa*. The shrine dedicated to Nandi is flanked by 51 feet high, great *dhvaja sthambha*-s or free-standing pillars, which are repeated throughout the complex relieving the denseness of the great stone temple.

It would take hours to explore the complex. One might easily lose oneself here. Each feature of the Kailashnath invites observation — its immense carved *dwarapala-s*, for instance, which recall the large statues of kings at Thebes in Egypt; its mammoth pillars that dwarf the visitor and must have taken an extraordinary amount of time and dexterity to create; its large tableaux depicting not only the legendary episodes from the life of Shankara but scenes from what the local artists might have imagined his daily life to be like. He sits, surrounded by his family, in an ancient group 'photograph' or spends his free time playing an ancient form of chess — *chausar* — with Parvati, his wife.

There are several panels depicting the demon-god, Ravana, who was Rama's opponent in the *Ramayana* but also a great Siva *bhakt* (devotee) who ultimately made the mistake of believing his powers could equal those of the great god. There are also colossal and impressive figures of elephants, lions and gryphons, vivid in depictions of battle or preying upon each other.

PANDHARPUR

Pundalik var de, Hari Vithal
(Pundalik, grant us a boon, Hari Vithal)
Pilgrim's chant

The god of Pandharpur lives in the land of the common people. Vithoba (Vishnu's local name, an affectionate form of Vithal), the village deity, has traditionally been the god of the masses, living like them, even looking and behaving as one of them rather than an awesome superior being. In the heartland of the *Bhakti* movement (which advocated intimacy or personal communion with God), Vithoba came down to earth frequently and interacted with his devotees in the Pandharikshetra situated on the southern bank of the Bhima river in the Solapur district of Maharashtra.

According to the annals of Pandharpur, many of the town's Vishnu shrines originated at the sites where the god gave his faithful followers a *darshan* (sight of god, Epiphany). Take the hut temple of Taak pithya Vishnu, for instance. Centuries ago, an old woman sought to visit the famous Vithoba shrine located in the most holy part of Pandharpur but could not reach it because of the hordes of pilgrims pushing to get in. For 15 days she waited in her hut, refusing to eat until she could offer Vithoba *taak* (buttermilk) and *pith* (flour, in this case, bread). Finally he took pity on her, coming to her humble home and allowing her to worship him there. Thus the hut gained importance as a holy *sthana*.

Vishnu's main abode, the Vithoba temple, is located in the centre of the raised, holy part of town. It is a short walk from the old woman's hut. Of uncertain date, it was probably a primitive shrine that was formally sanctified around the 12th century AD. Renovated and added to over the centuries, the temple is a hotchpotch of architectural elements. It can be entered from the river by way of a *ghat* where a brass plaque commemorates the *samadhi* (final resting place) of the well-known Marathi Vishnu devotee and poet, Namdev.

Apart from the main shrine, the Vithoba temple complex also contains a 16 pillared temple, a black stone Saraswati shrine and a *shejghar* (bedroom), complete with silver couch for the god. But what people really come to see is the temple's unique idol, probably sculpted not later than the 5th or 6th century AD. Vithoba, carved in polished black stone, is garbed in the regional dress, including the local headgear. He stands straight and tall on a brick, arms akimbo, waiting for the devotee to approach him.

The legend of why he is depicted on that brick is an engaging example of how myth has become connected with the region's history. Centuries ago, there lived in Pandharpur a caste-conscious Brahmin called Pundalik. He was selfish and rude, and a disobedient son to boot. One day he embarked on a *tirtha yatra* (journey of pilgrimage) to Varanasi, taking his parents with him.

On the way, his *chappals* (slippers) tore so he stopped at the home of Rudradas, a cobbler (traditionally considered low-caste), to have them repaired. Rudradas, engaged in serving his aged parents, asked Pundalik to wait. While he did so, the arrogant Brahmin noticed two beautiful women sweeping the cobbler's yard.

As soon as he had time, Rudradas mended the pilgrim's shoes but would take no fee from him. "You are on your way to Kashi, I see," he said. "If you would be kind enough to put this coin in the Ganga for me, I would be grateful." Pundalik agreed to do so. When he reached Varanasi he threw the copper in, remembering his promise to Rudradas. Suddenly the beautiful arm of a woman adorned with a gold bangle appeared out of the water. Pundalik took it to be a sign from God and removed the bangle to take back to the cobbler.

When he returned to Rudradas' home, he saw the two fair women again and realized that they were the river goddesses, Ganga and Yamuna, for one of them was missing a bangle, the very one that Pundalik had removed from the arm in the holy river. He was so impressed by the fact that goddesses themselves were serving Rudradas as reward for his great devotion to his parents, that he immediately repented his own unfilial attitude and vowed to turn over a new leaf.

Soon Pundalik became so renowned for his piety and dedication that people came from near and far to meet him and be blessed by him. His fame even reached Vithoba, who decided to pay the Brahmin a visit. But just as he had introduced himself to Pundalik, the Brahmin's parents called out to him from within the house. So greatly changed was Pundalik that, asking Vithoba to wait while he attended to them, he gave him a brick on which to stand.

So God stopped for man. And that's how patient Vithoba stands even today waiting for his devotees to have the time to come to him. In this unusual temple town, even the traditional pilgrim's chant *Pundalik, var de, Hari Vithal* (Oh Pundalik and Vithal, please grant me a boon), in which the invocation of man (Pundalik) precedes that of god (Hari or Vithal), reflects the synergetic relationship that mortals shared with the divine.

Five hundred yards east of the main Vithoba shrine, is one dedicated to Pundalik. Made of stone masonry, the structure consists of *garba grha* and *sabha* (council or gathering) *mandapa* and contains a smooth quartz *linga* protected by a black stone *shalunka* (casing). The temple is also said to contain Pundalik's own samadhi.

For five days in February and March, the Koli fisherfolk worship here singing *bhajan-s* day and night. Close by is the Lohdanda Tirtha (pond) where Pundalik gave up sin. Its waters are said to be so pure that even boats carved of stone float upon them.

Another temple immured in myth and mystery is the *Vishnupaad* (see Vishnupad, Gaya, Chapter 4), south of the Lohdanda Tirtha and set in the bed of the Bhima river. Notwithstanding the fact that it is submerged for three and a half months each year, this shrine is one of the most sacred *tirtha-s* in Pandharpur and the spot where Krishna and his companions celebrated his reconciliation (after one of his frequent quarrels) with Rukmini.

In the tiny central shrine are three rocks with six inch long indentations in them. People claim these marks to be the footprints of Vishnu's Krishna *avatar*. Apparently also visible are the hoof marks of his cow. The prints on one rock indicate that the god stood there, feet firmly planted on the ground.

According to prints on another, Krishna stood at this spot on his left foot, with the right one crossed over it and resting on his toes. This is an attitude in which he is customarily depicted in Hindu sculpture and painting; playing his flute and perhaps leaning against one of his faithful cows. Devotees worship at these rocks every afternoon and a clan of local priests called Badva look after the shrine and perform *pooja*.

The town of Pandharpur is filled with pilgrims all year round but becomes even more lively during the months of April, July and November when pilgrims gather from all over the state to take part in its religious fairs.

Aihole

There are approximately 70 shrines at the architecturally rich but relatively little-known village site of Aihole, in northern Kanara. Built between 450 and 700 AD, they prefigure later Chalukyan structures but are too experimental and tentative as yet to display any strong characterizing features.

Lad Khan

The most famous among these is an unusually named shrine, the Lad Khan. The 5th century temple derives its name from a Muslim hermit, Lad Khan, who lived in a hut close to it. It is a squat structure, only 50 feet wide, built on a high, wide stone platform, with a flattish, low tiered roof and uncluttered by other structures around. Prioritizing utility over ornamentation, it is spare and clean of line, consisting of sanctum, covered *mandapa* and square-pillared porch decorated with sculpture — the whole of it patterned on the square nine pillar plan dictated by contemporary northern design.

The hall is lit by means of wide stone grilled windows behind which is the circumambulatory. In the midst of this is a raised sanctum containing idols of the presiding deity, Siva, as well as carvings of river goddesses.

The slightly sloping roof of the Lad Khan is again typical of this early period where the practice of using timber for building was so common that though the roof here is of solid stone, its installment replicates tiles held in place by logs of wood angled over them. The tiered roof is 'broken' in the middle by a dormer-style window with an element of the *shikhara* in the way it draws the viewers' eyes heavenwards.

DURGA

This Brahmanical temple is a fascinating sight for, seen from a distance, it resembles the image of a *yoni* within which is set a Siva *linga.* An apsidal structure built on a high, moulded plinth, it is contemporary to, or slightly younger than, the Lad Khan. It is also a rare structure belonging to a short-lived experiment which attempts the curved plan of the Buddhist *chaitya* with a rounded end where the altar is located. In front of it is located a small, square altar probably used for the vehicle of goddess Durga, the tiger.

Sparely decorated, the shrine also possesses plain stone exteriors with some carving detail on the pillars of the gallery that surrounds the structure enclosing the *pradakshina* path. It is unlike later temples all over the country that utilized ornate external portions and austere interiors.

The inside of the Durga temple's verandah-like *pradakshina* path has decorative *chaitya* windows and is also carved with figures whose features one usually associates with Buddhist sculpture. In its rough-hewn style, the shrine greatly resembles the ancient rock-cut caves of Karli (Maharashtra) or Ellora, rather than the intricacy of free-standing stone temples. Its *garba grha* is topped by a short curvilinear *shikhara*, more in the Nagara style than the Dravida, with carved vertical segments protruding out from the curving building.

PATTADAKAL

From Aihole's early structures, the focus soon shifted to the modified shrines at Badami nearby but within a hundred years or so, around the mid-seventh century AD, building activity moved once more, this time to nearby Pattadakal. This site contains some of the most evolved temples of Chalukyan architecture, four in the Nagara style and the remaining six in the Dravida.

It is said that the craftsmen who built these temples were talented Pallava artisans brought forcibly to the site from Kanchipuram by Chalukyan conquerors during the founding of Pattadakal. The Chalukyan kings wanted to ensure the architectural splendour of their new kingdom. The use of the same artists would account for some of the similarities between structures of both regions. Indeed, the Virupaksha temple which supposedly inspired the creation of the gigantic Kailashnath of Ellora was itself derived from the temple of the same name at Kanchi.

VIRUPAKHSA

This Pattadakal shrine is the site's most renowned one for while many of the other shrines were failed attempts at experimentation with various styles, the Dravida Virupaksha shrine of Siva is not only well proportioned but refined. It is one of four great Saivite temples at Pattadakal, the others being the Papanatha (Nagara), the Sangameshvar and the Mallikarjuna (both Dravida). Virupaksha was constructed around 740 AD and its Pallava influence is visible in its plan and structural style, from the stepped *shikhara*, smaller than even the initial ones in Tamil Nadu, right down to the enclosing wall around the structure.

Still, the *gopuram*, nascent in the Kanchi structure, is missing in this shrine and though it retains much of the austerity of the earlier Aihole temples, it does also possess a substantial number of carvings on its walls, mouldings, pillars, brackets and windows. These are executed in the indigenous style of the Kanara region.

The shrine is fronted by a closed, many-pillared and intricately carved *mandapa* with recesses containing statuary separated by stone grilled windows. This hall is entered through a deep porch-like vestibule. A narrow strip of land separates the structure from the Nandi pavilion before it. This open canopy with massive round pillars and curving stone awning, resembling the silk or wooden *chatri* (umbrella/canopy) of kings, protects a large, highly polished, black stone bull.

Nandi can, from his vantage point, 'look' straight down the passageway and hall to ensure the safety of his Lord in the *garba grha*, built along the same axis as the subsidiary structures. The bull sits untiring, alert and concerned for his lord. Above him are several bells, new additions, of course, in imitation of some that must have hung there before.

An important Chalukyan site in Andhra Pradesh is that of Warangal, once the capital city of the Kakatiyas who ruled of much of that state from the 12th to the 14th century. Of the remaining temples there; the Bhadrakali, the Swayambhu and the Thousand Pillar, the last is also the most important. Unfortunately, visitors will need to employ all their faculties of imagination to envision its grandeur as the complex is in a reprehensible condition, with all but one shrine in ruins. Even the remains have not been spared by vandals.

Hampi

On his journey south to Lanka to recover his abducted wife Sita, the legendary hero Rama, accompanied by his brother Lakshmana, traversed much of the Indian subcontinent. Wherever he was thought to have stopped to rest or pray, a temple was constructed to mark the holy site. One such place is in the famed town of Hampi, the seat of the Vijayanagara kings (the most well known of these being Krishnadevaraya). During his reign, Hampi (and indeed the entire kingdom), located on the holy Tungabhadra river near Hospet in south Kanara, flourished, not only economically, but also in the fields of art, literature, music, and architecture.

The large capital was also renowned as an exceedingly sacred site, called Bhaskarakshetra because it had the rare honour of possessing shrines to all the gods of the holy trinity — Brahma, Vishnu and Maheshwara (yet another name for Siva). It was also called Kishkindakshetra and Pampakshetra, this last title probably being corrupted over the centuries to give the site its present name.

According to the *Ramayana*, Hampi was ruled in ancient times by the monkey brothers, Vali and Sugreeva. In a tussle for sovereignty, Vali drove Sugreeva out and he camped on

Hampi ~ Paradise of the Trinity

Hampi ~ Paradise of the Trinity

the renowned hill, Matanga Parvatam, with his small but faithful band of followers, amongst whom was Hanuman. When Rama and Lakshmana passed through the area on their way to Lanka, Sugreeva enlisted their help to regain his kingdom.

Rama killed the evil Vali, restored Sugreeva to the throne and gained, thereby, a group of loyal soldiers. Hanuman became his aide from that day forward. The company waited anxiously on the nearby Malyavanta Hill till news of Sita sent them off on their journey again. Various white streaks on rocks in the cave where Sugreeva hid Sita's jewels, are still considered to be marks left by her clothing. A huge mound of ash is thought to be Vali's remains.

The region is abundant in mystery and enigma. The ruins of the ancient capital, spread over 15.6 square miles and sprinkled with shrines from various eras, bring forth images of a bustling and prosperous city. Numerous travellers from around the world attempted to describe the wonders of Vijayanagara in vain. "The City of Bijanagar is such that the eye has not seen, nor ear heard of any place resembling it upon the whole earth," wrote the Persian traveller, Abdur Razzak in the 15th century; about 100 years later, a Portuguese visitor wrote, "The city is situated like Milan, but not in a plain...It appears to me to be a second paradise."

Today, we can only imagine its grandeur from the ruins, which itself is a statement of Hampi's glory. The homes of both rulers and ruled are gone. So are most of the fortifications and army buildings. The only structures visible in once-mighty Hampi are its religious ones. As temples came to symbolize wealth and power, more money, time and effort was spent on their construction than even on the private palaces of kings. While contemporary manuscripts or travelogues documenting different periods in Indian history might wax eloquent about the beautiful homes, promenades, pleasure gardens and public buildings that ancient cities possessed, the only current evidence of this lies in their places of worship.

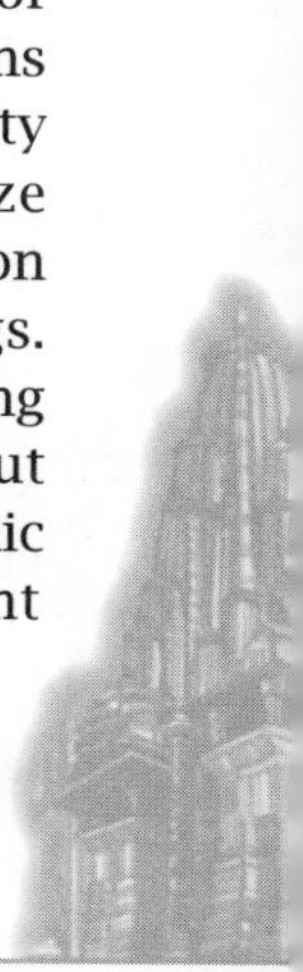

In Hampi these belong to several eras, the oldest being the pre-Vijayanagara temples, most belonging to the later

Chalukyan style. Two Devi shrines, some Jaina temples with stepped, pyramidal *vimana-s* on Hemakutam Hill, and a few around the tank of Manmatha Gundam, are from this period.

The Vijayanagara style, which grew out of the influential Chalukyan as well as the Tamil Pandyan traditions, came into its own over three centuries, from about 1350 to 1600 AD. It is distinguished by its highly ornate and intricate details in hard granite. Most of the temples of this period possess covered pillared halls, vestibules and circumambulatories and medium sized *gopuram-s*. But the showpiece of each temple is its collection of huge, finely carved, highly polished black stone pillars.

HAZARA RAMA

This now empty temple which once stood outside the north-western corner of the Hampi palace enclosure, was once thought to be dedicated to the Vishnu *avatar*, Rama. Its name may actually derive from the Telugu word *hajaramu,* meaning 'ancient hall'.

The Hazara Rama, 110 by 200 feet, was enclosed behind a high wall and consisted of a *garba grha*, several *mandapa-s,* including a large *kalyana mandapa* (temple hall where rituals such as weddings were held), used for the ritual marriage ceremony of the gods, and a number of porches. Facing eastward, with a decorated platform, the small but profusely decorated shrine had four of the noted Hampi stone pillars, decorated with images of Ganesha, Hanuman, the Vishnu *avatar*, and the Mahishasuramardini. Also embellished were its walls where episodes from the *Ramayana* are depicted.

SOMNATHAPUR

The Hoysala temple at Somnathapur, 27 miles east of Mysore, reflects the maturing of the Deccani style that was neither Nagara nor Dravida in ground plan and elevation. The entire complex was then constructed on an elevated plinth and corresponded with the plan of the star-shaped or polygonal temples atop it. Located within this plan were the *garba grha*, several *mandapa-s* and porches.

Chenna-Keshava

Indeed, this 13th century Keshava or Chenna-Keshava (small or baby Krishna) temple, epitomizes the pinnacle of Hoysala architecture. Though the smallest of that dynasty's temple complexes in the Kannada towns of Halebid, Belur and Somnathapur, it is the only complete one.

It possesses all the characteristics of Hoysala religious architecture; tiered platforms wide enough for circumambulation, intricate carved decoration, and the squat black 'lathe-turned' columns that appear almost as if they were made by machines, not human hands.

Chenna-Keshava is a complex of three main shrines, situated almost clover leaf in plan around an entrance *mandapa* with the famed columns, some of which are fluted. Also in the temple yard are 64 auxiliary shrines and, along its periphery, cloisters that face the shrine.

The beauty of this shrine is that there does not seem to be a single blank surface on its exterior. The outer walls and even the platform on which it is constructed are painstakingly carved — sometimes with canopies and awnings shielding an array of gods, dancers, and musicians, or tales from the two great epics; others, motifs of flora and fauna; yet others, documentation of contemporary pastoral life; and still more, rows of curlicues and other abstract design elements in constant repetition.

Note

1 The Buddhist cave site of Ajanta, about 20 miles from Aurangabad, Maharashtra, is well-known for its exquisite cave murals.

The Meenakshi Temple ~ Madurai

I am the God of the sensuous fire
That moulds all nature in forms divine:
The symbols of death and of man's desire,
The springs of change in the world are mine;
The organs of birth and the circlet of bones;
And the light loves carved on the temple stones.

Sir A. Lyall

The Meenakshi Temple - Madurai

I am the God of the sensuous fire
That moulds all nature in forms divine:
The symbols of death and of man's desire,
The springs of change in the world are mine;
The organs of birth and the circlet of bones;
And the light loves carved on the temple stones.

Sir A. Lyall

OF DIVINE VISITORS AND TEMPLE TOWNS

The Temples of the South

Tirupathi — Venkateswara; **Mahabalipuram** — Eight Ratha, Arjuna's Penance, Shore Temple; **Kanchipuram** — Kamakshi-Amman, Kailasanatha, Vaikunthaperumal, Ekambareshwara; **Tanjore** — Brihadishwara; **Madurai** — Meenakshi; **Rameshwaram** — Ramanathaswamy; **Kanyakumari** — Devi

On the heels of the Gupta dynasty of the north which contributed to the groundwork of Hindu art and architecture, a great ferment was taking place in the south. The major assimilation occurring here from the 5th to the 9th centuries AD, its 'golden age', was of the newer Aryan gods, ideas, and beliefs with the already present Dravidian religion and heritage. This osmosis resulted in a culture at once different from and similar to its northern counterpart. For, while retaining much of its vernacular Dravida tradition, it preserved the purest essence of the new art form developed in the north. With fewer invasions from the north into this peninsular area, there was little to distract or change its course.

South India is not just a land of temples but of temple towns with distinct deities and religious lifestyles. Most older urban centres in southern Andhra Pradesh, south Karnataka, Tamil Nadu and Kerala grew around temples. These were the focus of the local social and religious activity — *panchayat-s* met there, children were taught in their schools and the estates were often used for public fairs or entertainment like dancing or wrestling matches.

Festive occasions, ceremonies, daily rituals and calendars had been determined by religion in India for centuries. The south, however, brought a certain orthodoxy and rigidity to this interconnection. The system of caste became all-important across the country. It came to be observed with such Puritanism in the south, that its repercussions have led, centuries later, to a counter-discrimination against the upper castes, specifically Brahmins, in Tamil Nadu.

Southern temples belong, generally speaking, to the Dravidian or Dravida style. This evolved from the 5th to the 17th centuries AD under the patronage of powerful rulers, especially those like the Pallavas. This dynasty, the first great Tamil reign of the golden age, created the awe-inspiring but unpretentious Mahabalipuram. The later Vijayanagara kings built the great Karnataka city of Hampi.

Dravidian temples are essentially square in plan, strictly following the *mantra* (spell or invocation) of the old *Vastupurushamandala.* Their exteriors have pilasters, niches and other recesses and are usually heavily sculpted. Small, dark, sanctums are fronted by one or more *mandapa-s.* The spire of the southern tradition is pyramidal in form, divided into sections parallel to the horizon and topped by a circular (Vesara style) or polygonal crown.

A characteristic and famous feature of these shrines, the *gopuram,* actually exists outside the area of worship. It is the towered gateway that leads to the temple. Several storeys high, the *gopuram* probably developed from wooden structures of the same design. By the time the Dravidian style blossomed into an elaborate and elegant tradition, the use of great corridors and pillared halls had become prevalent. The greater the hall, the greater the temple. Yet, very often, the best known part of the temple would be the intricate *gopuram* which towered above the city signalling its location to worshippers faraway much as the church spire did in Christian lands. Another point worth noting is that while northern temples used predominantly vertical lines to uplift the devotee, the

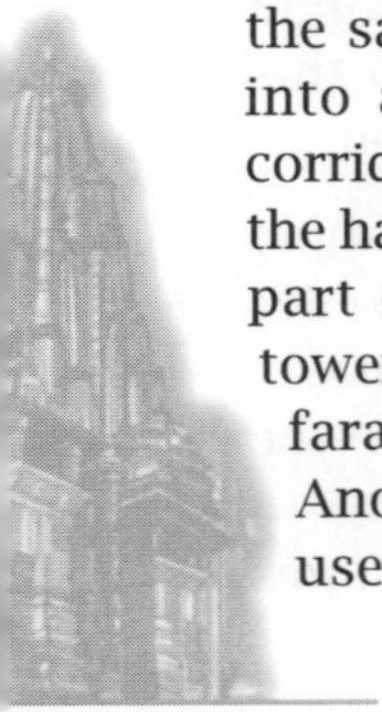

Dravidian utilized a horizontal line seen both in its mouldings and the many levels of its *gopuram*.

The periods of dynastic building in south India can be roughly demarcated as the Pallava (600-850 AD); Chola (900-1150 AD); Pandya (1150-1350 AD); Vijayanagara (1336-1565 AD); and the most recent, the Madurai phase (1600-1700). The effect of the Chalukyan builders of the Deccan was also felt in the region's architecture but their greatest works were, of course, distributed further north in the Deccan.

Also influential in the southern states were the Buddhists. As in other parts of the country, south India had been touched by the preachers of the Mauryan king Asoka. They travelled as far south as Ceylon and though they arguably made more of a lasting impression there (and throughout south-east Asia and the Far East), than in their motherland, important Buddhist shrines were built at Amaravati and Ghantashala and vestiges of their *chaitya-s* and *stupa-s* are seen in the barrel-style roofs of Mahabalipuram's shrines and in the domed crown placed on temple *shikhara*.

The names for Dravidian gods and goddesses also vary, in some cases, from those in the north. If we know some of these, the long complex names of temples become easier to comprehend. According to anthropologist Chantal Boulanger, "In the South, God is king. The words used to translate temple, 'koil' or 'kottam' mean, in fact, palace." [1]

"Perumal is the name of the Dravidian god who was assimilated into Vishnu."[2] He is locally known therefore as Venkatesaperumal or Srinivasaperumal or even by other names like Sri Balaji and Venkateshwara. In the south, Siva is often known by the name that denotes his role as the cosmic dancer, Nataraja. Krishna is Mayon in Tamil, Skanda is called Muruga, Somaskanda or Subramania, and Ganesha Vinayakar.

Separating fact from fiction is never easy. In the case of south Indian temples this is especially so. Many legendary rulers are said to have graced them with their presence. Which of these legends are true and which not, which kings were real and which mythical, cannot always be substantiated but the stories of their visits certainly add colour to the chronicles of each shrine.

VENKATESHWARA AT TIRUPATHI

This old anthill is the place where dreams come true. Atop a slope in the Mount Seshachalam range in the Eastern Ghats of India, Vishnu sat to meditate one day. He had left home because of a quarrel with his wife, Lakshmi. All he wanted was to be alone for a bit. So he closed his eyes and went into a deep trance.

The rain fell yet he did not move. The wind blew but it did not disturb him. Days, months, years went by. The animals of the forest began to think that Vishnu was just another rock on the hillside. Ants began to crawl all over him. Soon the god could not be seen. The busy ants scurrying to build a home for themselves before winter had buried him in the mud.

Vishnu meditated on. Until the day, a cow paid homage to him. As an amazed young cowherd watched, his cow walked straight up to the anthill and showered it with her milk. The boy told of the strange happening to his king, who, curious to discover the reason for the cow's behaviour, had the anthill dug up. Underneath he found Vishnu, literally turned to stone

. Ever since that day, the god has been worshipped there at what is now one of the richest and most commercialized shrines in India. Tirupathi — the meditating ground of Vishnu — is one of the 108 important Vaishnavite shrines across India; others include Tanjore, Kumbakonam, and Madura (Madurai).

According to another legend, the Venkatadri hills of Tirupathi represent the serpent, Naga or Adisesha, the vehicle of Vishnu, on whom he also rests. In a third tale, the hills are said to be a part of the holy Himalayan mountain, Meru. One day the god of the wind, Vayu, blew a mighty gust at Meru, scattering some of his peaks to the south-eastern part of the country where they formed the Eastern Ghats.

In the past, the five Pandavas came to these mountains, staying a year at what is now called Pandava Shringha, 'the place adorned by the Pandavas'. Rama is believed to have worshipped Vishnu here too. Today, thousands of devotees flock daily to the god's hilly abode to request that their dearest wish be fulfilled. In return, they offer up their hair at the shrine that was supposedly built by the Chola dynasty over the seven peaks of Venkatadri. In the foothills is a small altar dedicated to Govindarajaperumal. Beyond this is a tower built in honour of the wind, the Gali Gopura.

This gateway not only narrates through its carvings the ancient legends of the *Purana-s* but also documents history, for nearby is the figure of King Venkatpathy Raya, one of the great rulers of Vijayanagara. At the top of the hill is Vishnu's temple with its seemingly endless queue of pilgrims. All manner of *pooja* goods are available for his worship while pilgrims wait for hours, braving the heat and crowds, even ironically, paying a fee to catch a fleeting glimpse of the deity.

The idol of Venkateshwara they wait to see is squat like his Vamana *avatar*. His eyes are closed not only because he is meditating but because his gaze is so powerful it is said to scorch whatever it rests upon. Before the devotees realize it, the waiting is over, indeed they have been pushed by harried priests past the little figure almost hidden in gold ornaments. The *darshan* is complete. And they must be content.

On the same estate are some smaller shrines, one dedicated to Krishnadevaraya, the king responsible for the success of the Vijayanagara dynasty and who ordered the construction of many of the great buildings in his capital, Hampi. His wives, Tirumaladevi and Chinnadevi are also immortalized in stone in this structure.

Another small *mandir* has been dedicated to a minor god, Sudarshana, who is more commonly known as the weapon of Vishnu, the *sudarshana chakra*. He is also called Chakrapani and his fearful depiction consists of 16 arms, with weapons in each of them and a hexagonal flame all around him.

Where Vishnu once escaped to find peace and solitude among the mountains, there is now noise and bustle and money-making in what seems a travesty of worship. The god might have preferred to remain hidden in his anthill after all.

Mahabalipuram

Parts of this great port and capital city of the Pallavas who, at one time ruled the whole region from southern Andhra and eastern Karnataka down to Tanjore in modern-day Tamil Nadu, are believed to have been submerged by the ocean whose waves once lapped gently at its shores. It is intriguing to think that perhaps it was divine intervention that saved these magnificent temples though parts of the city itself were lost.

Most of the remains of the non-religious structures in the city indicate that they were made of brick and wood, and therefore perished. In its time, Mahabalipuram, now a quaint tourist centre situated close to Chennai, must have been a highly developed and beautiful metropolis with an adequate supply of water obtained from an efficient canal system.

Mamallapuram, as it was also known, was the site of the initial Dravidian experimentation in both rock-cut and free-standing temple architecture which set a precedent for the dynastic styles that succeeded it. The rock-cut style prevailed from the 6th to the 7th century A.D. With two variations, the monolithic *ratha*-s (chariots) at Mahabalipuram and its 10 *mandapa-s* — rock-cut, pillared halls — still nascent in style and similar to those of the Krishna, Guntur and Nellore districts and Tiruchirapalli.

Both belonged to the first phase of Pallava architectural development (the second consissting of the Mahabalipuram Shore temple and the Kailasanatha and Vaikuntaperumal shrines of Kanchipuram) but the former were probably models for temples rather than actual shrines in themselves and blatantly exhibit their Buddhist chaitya origins. They pre-date the Surya temple at Konark and perhaps inspired Bishu Maharana to build a chariot temple on a more grandiose scale.

THE EIGHT RATHA

The eight *ratha-s* in Mahabalipuram, commonly called the Pandava chariots or the 'seven pagodas', probably appearing as such from the sea, are better preserved than their Orissan 'replica', Konark. Being of one piece of stone, each carved from a half-mile long granite outcrop near the beach and another further south, about 250 feet in length, the former were in no danger of falling apart due to poor balance or shaky foundations (see Konark, Chapter 5).

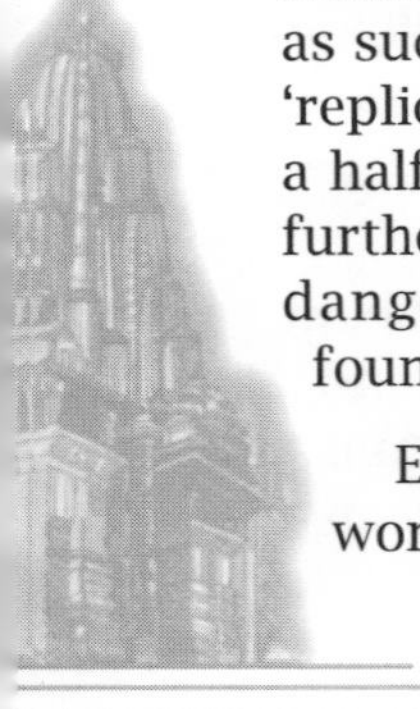

Erupting out of the ground, these early and relatively small works face different directions and vary from one to three

Mahabalipuram ~ Refuge by the Bay

Mahabalipuram ~ Refuge by the Bay

storeys in height. They prefigure various elements of the Dravida style of temple-building such as the two storey *vihara prasada* (sanctum sanctorum) and the *gopuram*. Indeed, the elevation and detailing of these shrines appears to be a direct ancestor of the south Indian temple gateways rather than the temples themselves.

The *ratha-s* include the Valaiyankutti and Pidari[3], a Ganesha temple and a small shrine to Durga, imitating perhaps a crude village hut or shrine and named for Draupadi, the wife of the Pandavas. There is also the similarly sized but two storey Nakul-Sahadeva *ratha*, with an 'elephant back'(humped) roof, which may be dedicated to Indra.

The three grand *ratha-s* of the older Pandavas were left in various stages of completion. These are the Arjuna, dedicated to Siva, now cracked down its middle; the Bhima shrine with its resemblance to a Buddhist place of worship — a barrel-like roof with curved vault and studded with small horse-shoe windows; and the three storey Dharmaraja (or Yudhishtira) *ratha* with its imitation of a thatched roof.

They all appear to be direct translations of local wooden architecture and the Buddhist stone style into an altogether new form from which the *gopuram* evolved centuries later. Around them are large carved figures of animals like lions (the Pallava symbol of power, repeated in all the Mahabalipuram shrines and in other Pallava cities) and elephants, rough-hewn but realistic in representation.

This quality of earthy realism is unique to Mahabalipuram. Though these shrines are some of the most primitive in the history of the south, their images may be more easily comprehensible to the modern viewer than much of the later work whose significance is lost in confusing symbolism.

At Mahabalipuram the positioning of the various sculpted characters, often life-size, is unconstrained. The motion of human limbs frozen in different acts is realistic — milking a cow, carrying another figure or a vessel, praying to god, holding up a draped *dhoti* to walk across the rock — and the expressions on their faces ingenuous. The proportions of animals like the elephant, the cow, the calf and the monkey are uncontrived and arguably far more beautiful than many examples of supposedly more sophisticated sculpture.

THE MANDAPA

This realism also extends to the *mandapa*-s. The 10 halls at Mahabalipuram are none deeper than 25 feet nor higher than 20. All are dedicated to Vishnu except for the Trimurthi cave. Though this last is ostensibly in honour of the holy trinity, Siva is given pride of place, appearing as the dominant central figure. A large Siva *linga* is set in the floor in front of the three-headed idol.

The other *mandapa*-s include those of the Pandava, the *Mahishasuramardini* (Durga) and Adi Varaha caves and although all possess massive and well-crafted pillars, they are but frames for the sculpted myths within. The first cave possesses a fine relief of the Krishna Govardhan legend, in which Krishna holds up the Govardhan mountain to protect his townsfolk who are shown engaged in the normal activities of dairy farming. A particularly fine detail is that of a farm hand, distinctly Buddhist by face and headdress, reverently bent before a cow, milking her while she washes her calf. The hand almost feels the soft fuzz on the calf's back, the tilt of the cow's head is so natural there would be no surprise if she suddenly turned and lowed.

THE SHORE TEMPLE (Alaivayakoil)

By the shores of Mahabalipuram is a stone temple complex that exemplifies the second phase of the Pallava style, with its shift from rock sculpture to free-standing structure. A pair of shrines is dedicated to Siva. The smaller one, with a relief of Siva, Parvati and their son, Skanda and a cell with a relief of a reclining Vishnu, is adorned by rows of gentle *Nandi*-s on its now-sunken walls, and overlooks the Bay of Bengal.

Built in the 8th century AD, the organization of the complex seems rather capricious as if the auxiliary structures might have been added later. The shrine itself is well planned, a modification of the Dharmaraja *ratha*, with a main entrance from the west and containing a *garba grha*, with an enclosing wall defining a *pradakshina* path and a small, partly closed porch. The stepped *shikhara* is similar to that of the Vaikuntaperumal in Kanchipuram and lends the temple a grace which heavier pyramidal spires lacked. The shore temple once exhibited great intricacy of detail in its sculpture but its fineness has been blurred by the wind, the salt air and the waves.

Arjuna's Penance Or The Descent Of The Ganga

What most people come to see at Mahabalipuram is not a temple but the relief carved on two gigantic boulders, one 100 feet high, the other 50 feet high, cleft in the middle. Often called 'Arjuna's Penance', it is actually the story of 'The Descent of the Ganga', telling how the river flowed powerfully down from the Himalayas because Bhagirathi, the sage, prayed to Siva to send water down to the needy earth.

Both rocks are filled with detailed carvings of vividly sculpted gods, men and animals watching the mighty river flow down. But the creators of this vast panel went beyond a simple stone representation and added spirit to the tableau by actually sending water gushing down the central cleft (from a hidden cistern placed above) towards which all the characters seem to move in a trance.

The shrines of Mahabalipuram leave one feeling overpowered by the innate strength of the dark, heavy stone and massive construction. However, there is also an enormous amount of energy, vitality and cheerfulness about its sculpture. The calm, down-to-earth depiction, not only of the scenes of daily life but also of the gods, brings the Pallava era alive for the viewer. One might be in a gallery looking at documentary photographs of the lifestyle of an unknown but seemingly peaceful and modest community.

Kanchipuram

The Kanchipuram of cotton fame and the Kanjeevaram of silk, this Tamil Nadu temple town of many names and many *gopuram*-s is one of India's *sapta puri*, considered by south Indians to be the most holy. For, of these seven cities, three are devoted wholly to Vishnu and three to Siva but Kanchipuram, the oldest of south Indian cities, is devoted to both.

The temple town has two distinct sacred zones — Vishnu Kanchi (the small town) and Siva Kanchi (the big town) and once possessed as many as 108 Siva temples and 18 Vishnu ones. Ironically, the shrine held most sacred by the local people, the Kamakshi-Amman is devoted to neither Vishnu nor Siva but to Siva's wife, Parvati.

The city's rich and long history tells us it was the capital of many of the great south Indian dynasties, the Pallava and Chola, and the kings of Vijayanagara, the latter two being responsible for much of the temple construction here. Legend also has it that Asoka was Kanchi's first ruler.

It was a centre of learning and worship not only for the two main sects of Hinduism — an important Shankara Math was located here till 1686 AD — but for Buddhism and Jainism too. Indeed, the 7th century Chinese traveller Hiuen Tsang records seeing a town full of *sangrama*-s (Buddhist enclaves) and a people "superior in bravery, learning, and piety to all the others [he] had met with in [his] travels all over India."

These superior people had created a town based entirely on the precepts of the *Vastu Sastra*, six miles in circumference, being occupied only by members of the Brahmin community. Even the king, being a Kshatriya, could not live here. His royal palace and the residential area for citizens of other castes was built outside Kanchi.

Kamakshi-Amman

In the heart of the city (situated 47 miles south-west of Chennai on the banks of the Vegavathi river), where a great many of its temples are located, stands Kamakshi-Amman. The striking structure with its large paved courtyard and famed golden *gopuram*, contains a depiction of the goddess as a *yantra* before whom a *chakra* (a geometric figure with mystical letters inscribed on it) is placed for worship.

The Kamakshi-Amman also contains a statue of the great philosopher, Adi Shankaracharya, who is worshipped there as a god. He brought about a revival of enthusiasm for the declining worship of the presiding goddess by apparently returning her power to her. This he is said to have done by

Kailashanath ~ Shrine of the Mountain Lord

Kailashanath ~ Shrine of the Mountain Lord

placing before her another geometric figure with the *Ashta Lakshmi* (eight Lakshmis) cut into it at the cardinal points. This is supposed to have renewed her energy. The temple estate also possesses the vital tank of purifying water and two small shrines; one to Vishnu, the other to *Annapurna* (the goddess of food and plenty).

The temple comes alive every February-March when on the ninth lunar day of the month a great 'car' (chariot) festival is held and Parvati is ritually bathed and adorned for the journey to her husband's home.

KAILASANATHA

The shrine of the Lord of Mount Kailash, Siva, is one of the oldest in Kanchi, commenced by Rayasimha, and completed by his son, Mahendravarman III, of the most ancient southern dynasty, the Pallava. Dating from the late 7th century AD, it is a rare example of the early Dravidian style for it escaped excessive renovation and addition unlike other unfortunate structures.

Kailasanatha was probably the inspiration for the Virupaksha temple at Pattadakal in the Deccan which in turn prompted the Chalukyans to build the monolithic Kailasanatha at Ellora. In a cloudless blue sky, baking in the hot summer sun, stands Kailasanatha, built of granite and sandstone, primitive and elemental in appearance. Its age is visible in its very stone work and sculpture, less refined, perhaps, but fresher and more from the heart than the convoluted and stylistic examples of the later Dravidian type.

There is more stone than carving visible in this low, spread-out shrine and the existing sculptures are not as intricate or as well finished as those of a later era. The *shikhara* above the sanctum is pyramidal but only four storeys high and with a gentle incline. The *gopuram* is also shorter and less well defined than it was to later become and its wagon-like top with domed finials bears a resemblance to the odd-shaped marriage lockets that south Indian women wear on gold chains around their necks.

Pilasters adorned with the Pallava emblem of the lion are as noticeable here as they are in their other famous capital, Mahabalipuram. Repeated all over the exterior of the temple, they resemble British heraldic symbols more than Indian temple motifs. The small temple was designed in totality rather than a series of thoughts and afterthoughts. Constructed within a high wall made up of pilastered niches, topped by cupolas, it advances the idea of an enclosed temple complex.

The entrances are on either side of the *gopuram*, flanked by eight chariot-like Siva shrines in the style of Mahabalipuram's Arjuna *ratha*. One passes under a thick stone awning to enter the courtyard. Within is a flat-roofed, many pillared *mandapa* and *antarala* leading to the *garba grha*. There are nine subsidiary shrines, integrated with the *vimana*, 58 more *ratha*-style Siva shrines on the back wall and three separate Vishnu, Brahma and Siva ones in the courtyard.

The sculpture at Kailasanatha borrows from fantasy unlike much of Hindu temple sculpture which is based on reality and the human form. There are odd-looking dwarves, gryphon-like creatures, 'gargoyles', and swirling stone adornment, especially evident in the *ghana dwara* (great door) of the main shrine.

Even the presiding deity is the strange hermaphrodite form of Siva, the Ardhanarishwara. This particular representation depicts the female half with a *veena* (string instrument) in its hand while the male half sits on Nandi, the bull.

VAIKUNTAPERUMAL

This Vishnu temple, similar to the Kailasanatha, was built soon after it, between 674-800 AD. Its patrons were the Pallava Parameshwara and Nandi Varman II. Though Vaikuntaperumal reflects the peak of the building style of that dynasty, it is a precursor of the thousand-pillar temples the Chalukyans so delighted in building.

The structure, more restrained and mature than the Kailasanatha, has a four storeyed *vimana*, 60 feet high, with a *garba grha* at each level. A seated idol of Vishnu is installed in the lower three levels and a Garuda in the topmost.

Each higher level is smaller in area than the one below it, giving the '*shikhara*' a stepped appearance, ethereal in effect.

The sanctum on the ground floor is enclosed by a *pradakshina* path and has stairs leading to the upper storeys where circumambulation was done on the narrow terraces. The shrine has cloistered walls with the imperial lion pillars of the Pallavas appearing, but less frequently. The back walls are ornately carved as is the rest of the temple, from the *shikhara* down. The *garba grha* is fronted by a closed *mandapa* rather than the earlier porch-like structures in vogue.

The Vaikuntaperumal is ornate but surprisingly unfussy in its carvings that are uniform and delicate. It exudes a sense of peace, with the sun creating an intriguing chiaroscuro in its deep cloisters, also echoed in the half white-washed, half dark stone structure.

Ekambareshwara

The most fascinating aspect about this large Siva temple is the story of its sacred mango tree. Locals claim it is 3,500 years old, and that Siva appeared to Parvati here after she prayed to him on the banks of the Vegavathi river. The spot where she prayed is also commemorated by a temple.

The holy tree has four branches that are supposed to represent the four *Veda*-s — *Rig*, *Atharva*, *Yajur* and *Sama* — and the presiding deity derives his name, Ekamranatha or 'Lord of the Mango Tree' from it. This deity once tested the faith of one of the simple but devout washermen (*dhobi*-s) of Kanchi, Tirukkurippuththonda Nayaka, by appearing to him as a poor, old Brahmin mendicant.

Nayaka was so devoted to Siva he spent all his time washing the clothes of Saivite pilgrims. The god-Brahmin gave him his dirty *dhoti* to wash, asking him to have it ready in time for the evening's worship, and Nayaka agreed. Then Ekamranatha hid the sun so the poor *dhobi* could not tell what time it was. Thinking it was already late and that he would be unable to have the *dhoti* cleaned as promised, Nayaka began to beat his head against his washing stone. Then did Siva appear before him and reward him for his piety and honour.

Commenced by the Pallavas but built by the Cholas, Ekambareshwara is set near a large *kund*, the complex being spread over nine hectares and containing a thousand-pillared hall entered by way of a *gopuram*. This and a huge stone wall were added to the temple by Krishnadevaraya as late as 1509 AD.

TANJORE

In the 9th century AD, the Chola dynasty defeated the last of the weakened Pallavas. They took over as the major ruling force in south India and one of their accomplishments was to elaborate upon the Pallava style of architecture. Tanjore, a rich temple town and the capital of the Chola kingdom located 218 miles south-west of Chennai, possesses the best monument to the skill of its architects — the Brihadishwara temple.

According to legend, in this ancient town, also ruled by the local Nayaka and the invading Maratha, lived a *rakshasa* (giant) called Tanjan, who was killed in battle by Nilamegaperumal, a form of Vishnu. As Tanjan lay dying, he begged that his home be named after him and so it was. This largely Saivite centre, renowned for its gold-work paintings and brass handicrafts, has over 50 minor temples but none the quality of the Brihadishwara.

The Cholas developed a style not only understated, utilizing plain exteriors but one that relied, unlike the Pallavas, on architectural detail. The lion emblem vanished, the use of pillars was refined, and bronze statuary incorporated to adorn shrines. Indeed today there are more examples of intricate and finely worked Chola metal figures to be found than those of their architecture, the only other important architectural sites being Darasuram, Gangaikondacholapuram, and Tribhuvanam. The Chola temples, with their semi-erotic sculptures, at Kumbhakonam, are also worth visiting.

BRIHDISHWARA

This exquisite temple labours under the misfortune of not being considered sacred in south India. The custom of only allowing high caste individuals into a shrine backfired on it.

Brihadeshwara, Tanjore ~ Majestic Monument to Divinity

Brihadeshwara, Tanjore ~ Majestic Monument to Divinity

Legend has it that the respected Saivite saint, Appar, was, for some obscure reason, not allowed to enter the shrine. He did not rant or rave in the manner peculiar to sages but walked calmly away, taking his revenge for the insult through silence. In his hymns, and therefore in the hymns of his followers, absolutely no mention was made of Brihadishwara. Ignored by the intelligentsia, it was bound not to receive acceptance by the common man.

So it stands, rejected and slightly forlorn, incongruously cheerful in colour, in a corner of a small fort in Tanjore. In the centre of a rectangular, walled enclosure measuring 500 feet by 250 feet is the Siva shrine, testimony to the wealth and power of the Chola monarch Rajaraja (the King of Kings) the Great. He reigned from 985-1018 AD and spent the last decade of his rule preoccupied with the construction of the temple.

It is surrounded by a number of shrines built to Subramania (Skanda), Parvati, and Thachanamurthy (or Dakshina Murthy — the god/idol who always faces south), at the cardinal points and protected by colonnades. The sanctum also has a series of halls — the *ardhamandapa* or vestibule; the *mahamandapa*; and the *Nandimandapa*, a pavilion dedicated to the Nandi bull.

The huge Nandi or *Swayambhu* (the self-created one), in this hall is carved from a solid rock of 'hornblendic gneiss'. It has been polished over the centuries into a deep, glossy black by gingelly oil, which is also used in local cuisine.

According to a local myth, a live frog resides within the Nandi. When the temple was first built, the bull apparently miraculously appeared from the ground and was of a relatively small size. However, he went on expanding, until the great king, worried that Nandi would dwarf his temple, ordered the frog within to be killed. The image was broken at the back and a sword put in to kill the offending creature. But he was hardy and though he stopped expanding, he is thought to be alive still for his blood supposedly continues to seep out from the crack in the stone.

The monumental entrance to the temple is between two

shrines to Siva's sons, Ganesha and Subramania (or Skanda as he is known in the north) above which rises up the 40 foot, five storey *gopuram*, whitewashed in customary fashion and embellished with coloured plaster figures and delicate fans, the archetype of the south Indian shrine. Two large and grotesque *dwarapala*-s guard the approach to the shrine. Depicted with four hands each, they tell the pilgrim, with the upraised forefinger of the lower right hand, 'Sinners may not enter here'. The open palm of the upper right hand warns, 'I smite those who disobey my order'.

Behind this entryway is a three storey, inner *gopuram* opening onto a clear courtyard, enclosed by a thick wall. This is topped with 1,008 Nandis. There are three subsidiary gates to the west, north and south, aligned with the centre of the sanctum. The open court leading to the main shrine is paved with brick and provides the space required to stand and appreciate the imposing building. Towards the back of the estate are a well and platform where dancing girls performed every April during the temple festival. The temple is not set in the exact centre of the yard but slightly back near the west wall. It faces the dawn and possessed a gold tipped dome, hewn from a single block of granite supposedly weighing 80 tons.

The simplicity of the Chola style of temple building is evident in the flat, dressed stones of the sanctum overlaid judiciously with decorative detail. Rising up from a high plinth and reached by way of stone steps, the shrine is built upwards in tiers, with the molding on each level accentuated by a simple, miniature horse-shoe pattern. Its recesses hold many statues of dancers, warriors and the *ashtadikpala*-s. As the hollow 16 storey high *shikhara*, also layered, begins to stretch towards the sky, it is beautifully adorned at equal intervals with the fan-like stone work of the Brihadishwara's *gopuram*, perhaps representing the vehicle of Subramania, the peacock.

MADURAI

One Monday (*Somava*r, the day of the moon, of nectar) evening, many moons ago, Dhananjaya, a merchant from Manavoor, was returning to his home after a long and arduous business trip to the west coast. Making his way through the darkening forest at dusk, he stumbled upon Indra, the god of thunder. Now Indra, who had in some way offended the mighty god, Brihaspati, was in the forest to atone for his sins. Here he sat and he prayed for forgiveness, on one full moon night a year (*Chitra Poornima*) to Sundaresvara (Siva; the beautiful god).

The holy sight of Indra worshipping the Siva *linga* elated Dhananjaya. He shared his story with his monarch who immediately ordered that a shrine be built commemorating the divine site. So workers cleared the woods, constructed a temple and built a planned city in the shape of a coiled serpent. They could not, however, find a fitting name for this new town. Then one night, the king dreamt that Siva was sprinkling sweet *madhura* (nectar) over it and so called it Madhurapura, the sweet town, later shortened to Madura and now known as Madurai. It was a part of the Pandya kingdom from the 12th to the 13th century A.D. and the 'seat of Tamil literature'. Literary conferences called *sangam*-s were held here and Siva is said to have even attended one as Sundaresvara, the poet. Here also, Parvati was born on the earth once more, this time as Meenakshi, 'the one with the eyes of a fish', the daughter of the local Pandya ruler.

The Pandyas did not contribute substantially to the evolution of Dravidian temple architecture for the strain of the expense and labour required for such constructions of magnitude, already ample in number, was beginning to be felt. Instead they and their successors, the Vijayanagara monarchs and the Nayakas, wisely decided to utilize resources to restore or embellish existing structures. Meanwhile, they directed their creativity towards the temple's environs — gateways, for instance, were less expensive to build than temples themselves. In the 13th century the *gopuram* rose to refined heights while in later years, elaborate complexes with all manner of facility (auxiliary shrines, accommodations, refectories, performance halls, infirmaries) were constructed in rings around the original shrine.

Meenakshi

Nevertheless, it was in this environment that the large, intricate, labyrinthine, and necessarily expensive temple complex was built to celebrate the marriage of the Meenakshi-Sundareshwara incarnations of Parvati and Siva.

Parvati, as the princess Meenakshi, was born with a peculiar deformity. She had three breasts. Her royal parents were naturally worried but a seer reassured them that as soon as the girl found the right husband, Siva, the third breast would disappear. Indeed, when Siva and Parvati were wed on the full moon day of the month of Panguni (February-March), it did disappear and the divine couple lived happily in their abode in Madura.

Their six hectare estate known as the 'twelfth place of peace' (Dwadasantham), has four high outer walls and stands in the heart of the city. Above it, the temple's 12 lofty *gopuram*-s rise skyward. Much of the enclosed space was rebuilt in the 17th century after its destruction by Malik Kafur who razed the walls and 14 original *gopuram*-s to the ground, leaving only the inner sanctums intact. The new structures were designed by Viswanatha Nayak in 1560 but erected between 1623 and 1655 AD during the rule of Tirumala Nayaka.

The Baroque-style temple contains not only a collection of shrines and cloisters but also *mandapa*-s — these include a *kalyana mandapa* where Siva and Parvati are ritually married every year and a 1,000 pillar hall (with only 985 pillars) built around the middle of the 16th century — tanks, chapels, palaces, altars and storehouses. It is a miniature, self-sufficient world.

The foci of this busy world are the shrines of the presiding deities, Sundaresvara and his wife. The altar of the former is forbidden to pilgrims and is cloaked in perpetual darkness. Nearby is a holy tank, the Maha Pathaka Tirtham, the waters of which are believed to cleanse the worst of sinners. Opposite this lie the ruins of an old Vishnu temple.

The shrine of Meenakshi is also dark like her husband's; framed by a golden door and reached by the *Ashta Sakti Mandapam* (hall of the eight goddesses or powers). The goddess's sanctum is protected by those of her sons, Ganesha on her right and Subramania on her left.

About three miles east of the temple is a 1,000 foot square, picturesque tank called the Vandiyur Teppakulam, connected to the Vaigai river by a channel. Like the Bindu Sagar in

Bhubaneshwar it has, at its centre, a square island with one main temple on it and four subsidiary ones at its corners. The tank has been held as sacred ever since a large Ganesha statue was discovered in its depths. The idol is now housed in the middle *gopuram* near the Siva shrine.

RAMESHWARAM

The island of Rameshwaram is one of India's four most holy tirtha *sthana*-s and frequently called the 'Varanasi of the South'. Located in the Gulf of Mannar en route to Sri Lanka (Ceylon) from India, the island, indeed the entire region, is steeped in the lore of the *Ramayana*.

At the Ramanathaswamy temple, Rama is said to have beseeched Siva to help him get back his wife, Sita. She was being held captive in Sri Lanka, by its *rakshasa* king, Ravana. Rama's prayers were soon answered. Not far away at the site of the Kothandaraswamy temple, Ravana's brother, Vibeeshana surrendered to Rama and joined the forces of good over evil. And Adam's Bridge, a string of reefs and islets that are almost stepping stones between the mainland and Sri Lanka, was supposedly built by Rama's aide, Hanuman, in order to reach the island and rescue Sita.

RAMANATHSWAMY

For Rama's devotees, the huge, almost cave-like Ramanathswamy (the lord of Rama) Siva temple is a must-see but both Saivites and Vaishnavites worship here, the temple being linked to Vishnu (Rama, as we know, is an incarnation of Vishnu) as well as Siva. However, only Hindus are allowed into the inner sanctum of the 12th century shrine. Although built over 800 years ago, Ramanathaswamy, a live temple that is a testament to the architectural skills of the Nayaka rulers, is famed for its great halls, massive pillars and rich sculpture has been added to and elaborated on over the centuries.

DEVI AT KANYAKUMARI

The land's end of India is a legendary spot for several reasons. Swami Vivekananda, the renowned religious

philosopher and freedom fighter meditated on the rocks here in 1892 and is said to have received divine knowledge. Tourists and followers of the Swami flock to the site where the landscape may be bare and arid and the atmosphere tawdry and frivolous, but the exquisitely tinted ocean more than makes up for these disadvantages.

In ancient times when the legend of the perpetual virgin was still fresh in people's minds, her home, Kanyakumari (Cape Cormorin) was a great centre of pilgrimage. Her temple, an unimpressive structure apparently reconstructed by the Pandyas in the 12th or 13th century, stands on the rocks today at the southernmost tip of the Indian peninsula overlooking the newer Vivekananda Memorial on the rocks across the strait. Meanwhile, she awaits her lover, observing wistfully the mingling of the lucid azure, emerald and aquamarine waters of the Bay of Bengal, the Arabian Sea and the Indian Ocean.

As most of the gods in the Indian pantheon occasionally descended from heaven to earth to protect mortals from evil, so did the goddesses. And when Vanasura, the demon of the forest, is said to have threatened the kingdom which stood where Cape Cormorin does now, the mother goddess Sakti (or Devi) came there, taking birth as the daughter of the local king.

As was common with goddesses and Indian princesses, she grew up to be a beautiful woman. And as was customary with Indian fathers, whether royal or not, the king started the search for a suitable husband for his young blossom. Since in heaven she was Siva's consort, he was the only man she could remarry. So the princess prayed to Siva on Mount Kailash to come down and wed her again at a particular *muhurta* (auspicious time, decided by the positions of the stars, for all Hindu ceremonies). Hearing her prayers, he awoke from his meditation and started the long journey to the south.

In the meantime, the other gods were worried. If the wedding took place, the girl would revert to her divine form and return home with Siva leaving the original purpose of her descent to earth to kill Vanasura incomplete.

So they conspired against their lord. The meddling sage

Narada followed Siva on his journey. Just before the god was about to reach Cape Cormorin, Narada crowed like a rooster. The puzzled Siva thought he had miscalculated the distance and that morning had already arrived. He had missed the *muhurta.* Shocked, he realized he could not now marry Devi. The spot where he stopped walking is marked by the beautiful Suchindram temple with its exquisite *gopuram* and carvings visible from afar.

Not many miles away, the lovely princess kept waiting, adorned with the clothes and ornaments of a bride. The town was festive for the royal wedding, flower garlands were festooned across streets, and platters of *akshata* (brightly coloured grains of rice) were kept by to shower the happy couple with. But Siva never came.

Vanasura, the demon did. So Devi did her duty and killed him, scattering the trays full of akshata in her wake. Then she waited again, but in vain. It is said that the faithful goddess stood there so long she turned into stone. That tragic stone figure is worshipped at the spot where she had pined for her divine lover. The akshata that had fallen unhappily around her also turned into stone. They are the little coloured pebbles visible even today on the rocky shores of Kanyakumari·

The princess, Devi was simply another incarnation of Sati whose body had sanctified the Indian sub-continent eons before. As the perpetual virgin, defender of her kingdom, Kanyakumari provided a reassurance to mortals that their land would always be hallowed and that the gods would inhabit it forever.

OM

Notes

1 *In The Kingdom Of Nataraja: A Guide To The Temples, Beliefs, and Peoples Of Tamil Nadu*, Chantal Boulanger, Tom Dawber, The South India Saiva Siddhantha Works Publishing Society, Tinnevelly Ltd., Madras, 1993

2 *ibid.*

3 There are actually two Pidari *ratha*-s at Mahabalipuram

GLOSSARY

A

abhanga — one of the four basic stances of human figures in Hindu sculpture, where there is a slight bend in the body
akshata — grains of rice used as confetti or in pooja
amalaka — dome or crown on temple's spire
amavasya — no moon night
amrit ghata — pot of holy nectar
Annapurna — the goddess of food and plenty
antarala — vestibule or porch. Also called *jagmohan* in Orissa
apsara — fairy or sprite
ardhmandapa — entrance porch, literally half-a-hall
Ardhanarishwara — hermaphrodite form of Siva, the half-woman god who represents the two aspects of human beings: the masculine and feminine, the passive force and the active
ashtadikpala — eight guardian gods: Indra, Agni, Yama, Nairita, Varuna, Vayu, Kubera and Isana
Ashta Lakshmi — eight Lakshmis
Ashta Sakti Mandapam — Hall of the eight goddesses or powers
asura — demon
atibhanga — one of the four basic stances of human figures in Hindu sculpture, excessive bend
avatar — incarnation. There are 10 avatars of Vishnu. These are: *Matsya* (fish), *Kurma* (tortoise), *Varaha* (boar), *Narasimha* (man-lion), *Vamana* (dwarf), *Parsurama* (Brahmin warrior), *Rama* (the ideal man), *Krishna* (the dark-skinned god, brought up as cowherd), *Bud*an avatar), and *Kalkin* (an amorphous avatar yet to appear)

B

Brhat Samhita — architectural treatise compiled by Varahamihira, in the mid-sixth century AD and based on the works of legendary architects like Manu and Visvakarma

C

cella - sanctum in Kashmiri temples
chaitya — large rock-cut temple for the worship of the Buddha
chakra — a geometric figure with mystical letters inscribed on it
chatri — umbrella/canopy
chausar — an ancient form of chess

chou-chala — style of roof in Bengal; here, a hipped roof with a square sanctum below it

D

darshan — sight of god, Epiphany
Deccan — Dakshin, south. The Deccan defines the geographic region that separates the northern and southern parts of India
deul - see garba grha
deva - god
devadasi - woman 'married' to god who danced in worship of him. Devadasis were literally the 'slaves of god'. The profession was hereditary and initially highly honored. In time it degenerated into prostitution thus taking on a negative connotation
devi — goddess
dham — centre of pilgrimage
dharamshala - accommodations specially built within temple complexes for visiting pilgrims
dhvaja sthamba — free-standing pillar
dhobi — washer man
dhoti — a piece of cloth worn by men, tied across the waist and tucked between the legs, forming trousers
do-chala — v style of roof in Bengal; here a pitched roof with a rectangular sanctum below it
Dravida — v a broad classificatory term for south Indian style of temple-building
dwarapala — doorkeeper

G

gana and yaksha — spirits of fertility and nature
gandharva — heavenly musician and dancer
garba grha — place of the womb and, therefore, sanctum sanctorum. Also called *deul* in Orissa, *mula prasada* in Rajasthan
ghana dwara — great door
ghat — mountains as in the Western ghats on the western side on the Indian peninsula and the Eastern ghats on the eastern. In this case, steps or a landing on a river
ghee — clarified butter used both in cooking and as an offering to the gods
gopuram — a Dravida temple's towered gateway
gridhamandapa — closed, central hall
guru — teacher

h

hans — swan

J

jagmohan — see *antarala*
Janmashtami — Krishna's birthday
jhanva — sacred thread
jivan mukti — salvation and, therefore freedom, gained during one's lifetime
jogi — mendicant
jyotir — the light/the lit one. Here, one of 12 special, sacred Siva lingas in the country called jyotir lingas. The others are located at: Srisailam; Ujjain; Devgadh; Rameshwaram; Bhimashankara; Triambak, near Nasik; Grishneshwar, near Ellora; Kedarnath; Kashi; Mandhata; Darukavana

K

kalyana mandapa — temple halls where rituals such as weddings were held
Kama Sutra — Kama, the god of love, sutra - rules, therefore, the rules of love. A guide to the pleasures of physical love, compiled in the 4th century A.D. by Vatsyayana
kshetra — ancient region believed to have active, divine power
kumbha — pot
kund — water tank

L

linga, Siva linga — phallic symbol, the male element, revered as the source of life

m

madarsa — Islamic primary school
madhura — nectar
Mahabharata — one of two great Indian Vedic epics, it consists of 10,000 verses and is the story of the Bharata dynasty that gives India its local name, Bharat. It tells the tale of the great battle between the Pandava and Kaurava brothers and was written in the early to middle part of the last millennium B.C., prior to the *Ramayana*
Mahadeva — another name for Siva
mahamandapa — grand or main hall

Mahasivaratri — the birthday of Lord Siva
mandapa — closed or pillared hall in temple, literally, a pavilion, meant for congregational activities
mandir — temple. Other terms used to denote a temple include *vimana* (well-proportioned), *prasada* (seat of the Lord), *devalaya* (house of God), *devagram* (the village of God), and *sthana* or *sthanam* (the holy place)
manastirtha — pilgrimage of the mind
mantra — spell or invocation
math — centre of learning
matrika or *sakti* — mother goddess
Mayamata — ancient architectural treatise
mela — fair or festival
moksha — salvation
muhurta — an auspicious time, decided by the positions of the stars, for all Hindu ceremonies and rituals
mula prasada—see garba grha

N

naga or nagini — male and female snake or serpent; snake god and goddess
Nagara — metropolitan or fashionable, a broad classificatory term for the north Indian style of temple-building. Also called Indo-Aryan
nagini - see *naga*
namaskar — attitude of prayer, both hands folded to god
Nandimandapa — a pavilion dedicated to Siva's vehicle, the Nandi bull
naos - hall in Kashmiri temples
Nataraja - Lord of the dance, another name for Siva, the dancing form of Siva that performs the cosmic dance or Tandava Nritya
nat mandir — dance hall
nava graha — nine planets
nav kanyaka - the nine maidens, the nine holy rivers, including the Ganga and Yamuna
nav rasa — the range of feelings, of the gods and humans, classified as the nine emotions. These include *srngara* (erotic), *hasya* (laughing), *karuna* (pathetic), *vira* (heroic), *raudra* (furious), *bhayanaka* (fearful), *bibhatsa* (loathsome), *adbhuta* (supernatural), and *santa* (peaceful)
nava or *dasa tala* — the height of nine or ten lengths prescribed in ancient texts as the lengths of face and body to carve figures

O

oriel — window protruding out from the main structure like a balcony, heavily carved

P

pitha — place, in this case, holy place
pradakshina path — circumambulatory path
panchayatana — a five shrined complex where the central temple is surrounded by one at each of its corners at the cardinal points
pith — flour, in this case, bread
pooja — worship
Puranas - ancient stories. As opposed to Vedic literature, the Puranas contains traditional history and lore, collected in the millennium from 500 B.C. to 500 A.D.

R

Raja — king
Rajtarangini — the historian, Kalhana's renowned 12th century text on Kashmir
rajrania — In Orissa, the name for a yellow sandstone
rakshasa — giant, with a connotation of evil
Ramayana — one of the two great Indian Vedic epics, it is the story of King Rama, a Vishnu avatar and an ideal king and man. Written in the early to middle part of the last millennium B.C., this legend is still told, with regional variations, all across south-east Asia
Rani — queen
ratha — chariot

S

sabha mandapa — council/gathering, therefore congregational hall
samabhanga — one of the four basic stances of human figures in Hindu sculpture where the weight of the body is evenly balanced
santa — the benign or peaceful aspect of god
satya — truth
saras — swan
saptpuri — seven, ancient cities: Ayodhya (Oudh), Mathura, Maya (Hardwar), Kashi (Benares), Kanchi (Kanjivaram), Avantika, and Dvaravati (Dwaraka)
stupa — commemorative receptacle of Buddha's relics
sangrama — Buddhist enclave

sangam — ancient literary conference
sastra — treatise, science
shalunka — casing or sheath, covering
shejghar — bedroom
shikhara — spire
shilpin — artisan
sisya — student
sthambha — positions from the Kama Sutra
sudarshan chakra — discus
Swayambhu — the self-created one, in this case, the Nandi in the Brihadishwara temple, Tanjore

T

taak — buttermilk
Tandava Nritya — the cosmic dance or dance of destruction that Siva, in the form of Nataraja (Lord of the Dance) performs
Taptapani — the name of a hot spring in Kashmir; literally, boiling water
tirtha — pilgrimage or place of pilgrimage, depending on usage
tirthankara — saint of the Jaina religion
tirtha yatra — pilgrimage, journey of
torana — garland, gateway, door ornamentation
tribhanga — one of the four basic stances of human figures in Hindu sculpture, a triple bend
Trimurti — three idols, spelt Trimurthi in South India. Refers to the holy trinity of Brahma, Vishnu and Maheshwara
tri ratha — triangular shaped
trishul — trident
tulsi — sacred basil

U

Upanishads — mystic Vedic verses composed from c. 700 B.C. onwards
ugra — the enraged or terrific aspect of god

V

Vastupurushamandala — the ancient Hindu architectural principle, the diagram of a temple defined in a *yantra* or spell
Vastu Sastra — the 'science of architecture'
Vedas — *Rig, Atharva, Yajur and Sama* - the four Vedas or Vedic texts of Hinduism. "Our earliest literary source is the Rig Veda,

parts of which were originally composed prior to 1,000 B.C. The remaining Vedic literature (the other 3 Vedas) is of later date." The History of India, Romila Thapar, Volume I, Penguin India, Calcutta, 1990. The word Veda derives from the Sanskrit *vid* - to know. The Rig Veda consists of 1028 hymns to various deities and is the oldest religious text in the world.

veena — string instrument
Vesara — a sub-category of the Dravida style of temple building
vihara prasada — sanctum sanctorum (South India)
Vishnupad — Vishnu's foot; Vishnupaad, regional variation; in Pandharpur considered to be Krishna's foot
vimana — tower
vishram — rest/repose

Y

yagna — sacrifice
yaksha — see *gana*
yantra — spell
yogini — priestess
yoni — the female symbol - counterpart to the *linga* or phallic symbol

Z

ziarat — pilgrimage or visit to a shrine, in this case, a pilgrimage centre

Select Bibliography

Boulanger, Chantal & Dawber, Tom; *In the Kingdom of Nataraja: A Guide To The Temples, Beliefs and Peoples of Tamil Nadu*; The South India Saiva Siddhantha Works Publishing Society, Tinnevelly Ltd., Madras, 1993

Buitenen, J. A. B. (Translator); *Tales of Ancient India*; Phoenix Books, University Of Chicago Press, Fourth Impression, 1969

Cousens, Henry, MRAS; *Somnatha and Other Medieval Temples in Kathiawad*; Archaeological Survey of India, Vol XLIV, Imperial Series, Calcutta, 1931

Craven, Roy C.; *Indian Art*; Praeger, New York, 1976

Edwardes, Michael; *Indian Temples and Palaces;* Hamlyn, Great Britain, 1969

Fletcher, Sir Bannister, CBS; *A History of Architecture*; Eighteenth Edition, First Indian Edition, New Delhi, 1986

Kramrisch, Stella; *The Hindu Temple*; University of Calcutta, 1946

Mitra, Debala; *Pandrethan, Avantipur and Martand*; Archaeological Survey of India, New Delhi, 1977

Michell, George; *The Hindu Temple — An Introduction to its Meaning and Form*; Icon Editions, Harper and Row Publications, Great Britain, 1977

Nautiyal, Govind Prasad; *The Call of Badrinath*; The Fine Press, Lucknow, 1950

Radice, Betty (Editor); *Hindu Myths*; Penguin Books, Great Britain, 1978

Tadgell, Christopher; *A History of Architecture in India*; Viking, Hong Kong, 1990

Thapar, Romila; *The History of India, Vol. I*; Penguin India, Calcutta, 1990

India Travel Survival Kit; Lonely Planet Publications, Hong Kong, 1993

Acknowledgements

This book would have remained unfinished without Sanjiv Bajaj's encouragement, Sameer Marathé's help and Jerry Pinto's sense of humour and incisive editing. To all three, many thanks.

My thanks also to Chandralekha Maitra and Sharada Dwivedi for giving me the opportunity to write this book and to the staff at the Heras Institute, St. Xavier's College, Bombay, for their cheerful assistance.

I am grateful to my grandfather, S. C. Marathe, a treasure trove of knowledge and insights, and to Bruce Fleming for being a GPWB.

Also to all my friends, especially Leena Pandit, Sameera Khan, and Jagruti Gala, without whom little would be possible.

Most of all I thank my parents, Sudhakar and Meera Marathé, and my maternal grandfather, Anna.

This book is for them.